The Forgotten Prince

By

Leah Toole

The Forgotten Prince

Copyright © 2023 Leah Toole. All rights reserved.

All rights reserved. No part of this publication may be reproduced, stored, or transmitted in any form or by any means, whether electronic, mechanical, or photocopying, recording, scanning, or otherwise without written permission from the author.
It is illegal to copy this book, post it to a website, or distribute it by any other means without permission.

Also by Leah Toole

The Tudor Heirs Series

I – The Saddest Princess

...

II – The Haunted Queen

...

III – The Puppet King

...

Praise for the Novels of
The Tudor Heirs Series:

"I was blown away by Leah's take on Queen Elizabeth I. It gave insights and perspectives I had not read before. Brilliant author who has a deep understanding of Tudor history."

- USA

"There are many adaptations about the life of Queen Elizabeth I, but with this new book, Leah Toole still manages to convey new aspects and interesting information for me in an exciting way. My recommendation: have tissues ready…"

- Germany

"Absolutely adored 'The Saddest Princess' about Mary I. It was so well-written, and such a gripping read. I read it all in one go, and it's the best book I've ever read. Many thanks to the author for writing this masterpiece!"

- UK

"If you are looking for a book that will get you hooked into the Tudor world without making you feel like an idiot, this is the book. Leah Toole has such a gift to get the reader invested in the story and make history fun. If you are interested in the Tudors, I would highly suggest you read these books."

- Canada

I dedicate this book to mothers who have experienced loss.

Prologue:

Katherine

1st January 1511

It has been eighteen months since my marriage to Henry VIII. In that time, I have experienced indescribable happiness…but also unimageable grief.
But my pain will surely be repaid. God will see to it.
After one final push, I fall back against the sweat-soaked pillows just as the midwife holds up my wriggling babe like a prize.
Its skin is pink and bloody, its face squished together in an angry grimace.
But it is perfect, I can see that from the look of utter joy on the midwife's face.

"Ten fingers, ten toes, and – by the sound of it – a healthy pair of lungs," the midwife tells me triumphantly, as though *she* had just birthed it.

"But more importantly," she says as my ladies approach her to take a peek at my child, "it is a boy!"
I breathe a laugh as relief washes over me at the news, and I can finally allow myself to relax.
The midwife wraps my screaming newborn in a blanket then while my ladies *ooh* and *ahh* over the midwife's shoulder.

"A healthy boy, your majesty," the midwife tells me again in confirmation, a great toothy smile splitting her face.
I nod and hold out my arms, my breath still heavy as I try to regain my strength.
As the midwife places my son in my arms, I realise it had all been worth it. The pain, the worry, the fear…
Above all else, the *fear* had been the hardest part of this labour.

Fear that it would end as tragically as the last time.

When…

I shake my head. I should not taint this moment with the memory of the one who had come before.

The girl that had been born sleeping.

This moment is a triumph, however, brimming with utter contentment and pride.

My child. A healthy, living son.

I thank God for His watchful gaze over me, and that He saw fit to grant me this joyous gift – an heir for my husband, the King of England, and a child for me to love for the rest of my life.

God has saved me. I know He has.

For to have been met with yet another lifeless baby would have surely killed me.

52 days later…

22nd February 1511

I feel as though I've died…
I might as well have.
Never have I felt such hollowness. Such emptiness. Such *grief*.
I thought I knew of it. How wrong I was…for that was *nothing* compared to this.
I feel as though I am dead, and I almost wish I was. For then at least, the pain would end…
Our beautiful, perfect son…is gone.
God has called him to Heaven. But I wish I could have beseeched the Lord to have taken me in his place…and I would have *gladly* given my life in his stead.
We had named him after his father. Henry.
But I had always called him baby Hal.
He had been granted the title of Duke of Cornwall upon his birth, and he would have been the future King of England, had he lived.
His name had been Henry.
And though he has passed on, I beg of you…
Please…remember my son.

Chapter 1

April 1502
Richmond Palace, Surrey

Queen Elizabeth of York stared at the messenger in shock and horror before doubling over with a hand pressed to her chest.
She felt as though she had been winded, her breaths failing to go in or out as the news of her eldest son's death was broken.
Arthur.
Her first born…the Prince of Wales and future King of England, was dead.
Just like that.
Her husband, King Henry Tudor, who stood beside her just as stunned at the awful news, was the one to break the silence.
"What of Arthur's bride, the infanta of Spain?" he stuttered, "Is she…?"
Elizabeth of York could hardly believe her ears. How could her husband be thinking of anything or anyone else when their beautiful boy – their perfect heir – had been struck down by the sweating sickness.
"Princess Katherine of Aragon has not yet succumbed to the illness," the messenger told them, "There is still hope."
Queen Elizabeth's vision blurred then and her head felt heavy. She pressed a hand to her mouth to stop herself from being sick.
Hope.
There was no more hope.
Not now that her precious boy was no longer with them.
Arthur had been the most beautiful of babies. From the moment he had been born fifteen years ago, Elizabeth had known that he would have made an incredible King of England.

Her love for her firstborn child had, of course, fuelled these feelings initially. But as the years had gone by, Arthur had proven himself to be as gentle, kind, and selfless as Elizabeth had predicted he would be.

Queen Elizabeth had borne her husband three more living children after Arthur's birth, all of which she loved more than life itself.

But Arthur had always been special.

Perhaps it had been due to him being her first child, the one who had turned her into a mother.

Or perhaps it was that he would have been Henry's heir, the one to take over as king and to one day rule England in his father's stead.

The queen had debated these different possibilities for many years.

But now that news had come that her beautiful boy was *dead,* Elizabeth could finally admit what she had always known in her heart: that Arthur had been her favourite.

A good mother would never reveal this of course, and especially now in death she would not. For she would need to pour all her residual love into her three surviving children.

Specifically, the only other boy that remained to take Arthur's place as Henry VII's heir.

This boy had not been brought up to rule as monarch, for he had been but the second son.

The spare.

The failsafe.

And now this boy would need to be hastily shaped into England's future king – a task which Arthur had taken on so easily, since he had quite literally been *born* to rule.

But this second son had been left to childish things much longer than Arthur had been. He had been allowed to get away with far too much in fact, leading him to have become selfish, spoiled, impatient…

He is but ten years old, Elizabeth told herself then, in an attempt to soothe her troubled mind.

It was true, there was time yet to mould the boy into a fine young man – a fine young *king*.

She would grieve Arthur – her favoured boy – forever, of that Elizabeth was sure…

But though one of her children had died, she was still a mother – and a queen – and she would need to show strength in this time of great, public mourning.

She straightened up then, swallowing the acid that had risen in her throat and blinked away the tears.

Arthur would have been a benevolent king, Elizabeth had known this from the moment he had been born.

But now that future was gone. And she could do nothing but hope that Prince Harry would grow up to become benevolent in his brother's stead.

May 1502

"We can have another," Queen Elizabeth of York said to her husband one evening as they shared a private dinner in the king's chambers.

It was a chilly Spring evening, even with the fire lit behind them. In fact, Elizabeth had believed it had felt notably colder ever since Arthur's death, as though his passing had sucked the warmth right out of this world.

Henry Tudor put his cup of wine down slowly and licked his thin lips, "We have Harry," he said matter-of-factly.

Elizabeth exhaled through her nose, "But what if –"

She couldn't say it. She could not voice the possibility of another child dying.

But her husband understood her worry, because losing a child – especially one who had overcome the dangerous years of infancy – well, it changed a person. And he and his wife, both, were understandably more concerned for their dynasty's future.

"Our only remaining heir is but ten-years-old," Elizabeth continued, her pleasant face burdened with worry, "we should at least consider having another spare."

Henry VII shook his head; he did not like it.

Though she still looked as beautiful to Henry as the day they were wed, at the age of thirty-six, Elizabeth was no longer in her childbearing prime, and to attempt to have another child would prove to be dangerous.

He took her hand and squeezed it, "It would be unsafe."

Elizabeth hung her head and picked at her flavourless food.

Normally, the queen would never counter her lord husband's final say – she was known to be soft-spoken, loyal, and gentle, a true princess of the blood – but on this matter, Elizabeth could not accept her king's ruling; for she needed to make sure England would remain safe throughout the next generation.

Her marriage to the Lancastrian Henry Tudor had united the two warring houses of York and Lancaster after three decades of civil unrest over the crown – the Cousin's War.

And she could not allow the country to descend into discord and bloodshed once more.

In case Harry, too, should die, England would need another male heir of the house of Tudor.

"My lord," she said, her voice pleading as she looked across the table and into Henry's eyes, "I beg you to do this for me. Let me give you another son."

February 1503

Prince Harry was but eleven years old when his mother, the beautiful and gentle Queen Elizabeth of York, tragically died in childbirth the following year, in an attempt to give her husband and king another son to replace the one they had lost.

She had birthed a tiny, premature daughter instead.

And it had all been in vain, for the baby, like her mother, died shortly after her birth.

The short-lived princess had been swiftly baptised Catherine – after the Spanish *infanta,* Katherine of Aragon herself, whom Harry's noble mother had cared for like a daughter since her arrival in England nearly two years ago.

Prince Harry – having been generally carefree for most of his life – had never deliberated the topic of death quite so much as he had done in the past year since his older brother's passing.

And now, with the demise of his beloved mother and baby sister so soon after Arthur's, it seemed death was the new foundation of all his thoughts.

Since Arthur's passing, Harry's life had ceased being carefree, for it had seen to not only the burial of his brother, but also to that of the life Harry had planned out for himself as the spare son – where he would have pursued the life of a man of the church and served God.

Instead, he had suddenly been forced down a path he had never even considered possible before, a path towards becoming the new Prince of Wales, and the future King of England.

But those had always been *Arthur's* titles.

And Harry's had been…well…Prince Harry.

He had obtained many other titles along the way of course: Duke of York, Warden of the Scottish Marches, Earl Marshal of England…

But none had weighed quite as heavily as this newest title did.

Prince of Wales.

It felt like it weighed a tonne.

And yet, though he mourned the death of his brother still, almost a year later, no amount of grief could have prepared him for the emptiness and heartache he had felt at the death of his beloved mother.

And Harry blamed no one but *himself* that she had died.

It hadn't been obvious to him when Arthur had been alive. But in the weeks and months that had followed his demise, Harry had noticed a shift in his relationship with his parents. At first, he had put it down to grief. After all, everyone kept telling him that that kind of sorrow could change a person.

But after some time, Harry realised that it had been more than that.

The issue was plain and simple: Harry was not Arthur…

If only he had been more like his older brother. More learned. More compassionate. More *kingly*.

Perhaps then his mother would not have needed to bear her husband another son. A better son than he…

And now, as eleven-year-old Harry wept miserably into his dead mother's bedsheets, he was suddenly certain that his parents had no faith in him.

And that their need for another son had no doubt been spurred on by their belief that Harry was not cut out to rule the kingdom.

March 1503

"You must eat," a familiar voice called from the threshold of the king's chambers, a voice which equally soothed and irked the newly widowed King of England.

"Mother," Henry VII exhaled irritably as he shook his head, his shoulder-length greying hair waving to-and-fro, "Please, leave me."

Margaret Beaufort did not do as her son and king had asked of her, and instead she took the silver tray of food from the servant by the doorway and walked towards her grieving son. She placed the tray down gently on the wooden table before taking a seat beside him.

"You must eat," she repeated tenderly, dropping her head to try to make him meet her eyes.

It had been but a month since the queen's passing, and Margaret Beaufort's sharp eyes could see that her already-thin son had lost too much weight in his grief.

Henry Tudor lifted his gaze slowly and blinked, to which fresh tears dropped to the stone floor.

"Mother," he whimpered then, his face crumbling with anguish, and he leaned forward for his mother to hold him.

His face was etched with lines and his beard was speckled with greys and whites, but the great King of England was still Margaret Beaufort's baby. He always would be.

Though Margaret had never been madly in love, as her son so clearly had been with his wife, she could still sympathise with his sorrow. For she could not even imagine losing *him* – her child – nevermind losing him and then losing the love of her life just a year later.

The monumental amount of grief that Henry Tudor was feeling of late must be insurmountable.

But she would do all in her power to help him overcome this. She would hold him and rock him, as a good mother should, and she would be there for him in this troublesome time.

April 1503

"The marriage between Arthur and Katherine had been meant to solidify our alliance with Spain," one of the king's members of the Privy Council reminded him one day at the king's regular council meetings, "Without their union, the alliance is left incomplete."

Henry Tudor exhaled loudly and rubbed his fingers back and forth across his forehead as though he would erase the last year from his mind, "The marriage took place," he replied, "The alliance is concluded. It is not England's fault that Arthur –"

He stopped short, still unable to utter the words.

The many men hung their heads at their king's inability to voice his troubles.

But then someone cleared their throat, hoping to move past the moment of silence and back to business.

"Isabella de Castille and Ferdinand de Aragon are not satisfied," an advisor added, "They will surely wish for their princess to return to Spain now that her year of mourning is over."

"Return to Spain?" Henry parroted then, his brows twitching, "They have not yet paid England her full dowry for her marriage to Arthur. If they wish for her to go back, they must conclude their side of the bargain."

"My lord, if I might be so bold?" one of the men, Edmund Dudley, said then as a thought came to him, "But Your Grace and the Dowager Princess Katherine find yourselves in similar situations. Both tragically widowed and in need of what the other can offer."

Henry raised an eyebrow and sighed, "Speak plainly, for the love of God…"

Edmund Dudley licked his lips, "If Your Grace were to take the Dowager Princess as your wife, then Spain would see their princess on the throne of England, and England in turn would receive the rest of her dowry as well as a finalisation to our treaty."

The council chambers fell silent for a moment while the idea was pondered, Henry trying to decide whether to laugh aloud – for surely it must have been a joke – or whether to scold the man for suggesting such folly.

But as the advisors all turned to look at their king, Henry realised that Edmund Dudley had been serious, and the thought of marrying another after his beloved wife's passing turned Henry's stomach in knots.

"Your majesty!" his mother's voice called frantically then as the doors of the council chamber were suddenly burst open.

"I bring news!" Margaret Beaufort announced as she hurried towards the men, flapping a folded letter in her hand, "From Spain. They propose that the *infanta* be betrothed to Prince Harry to maintain our alliance."

Margaret beamed at her son, her crooked teeth flashing victoriously at the great news that England's treaty with Spain might yet be saved.

And Henry Tudor was surprised that he had not thought of this solution himself.

The king sat forward and cleared his throat.

"Gentlemen, your proposal was…interesting. However, as you can see Spain has other ideas. And I have no doubt they would not have wanted to shackle their young princess to an old king like me."

Murmurs of disagreement began to bubble among the council, but the king continued, indifferent to their flattery.

"Spain puts forward an interesting alternative," Henry VII said, taking the letter from his mother's outstretched hand.

"But Prince Harry is only eleven years old," one of the members of council countered, "It would mean waiting years before the treaty is finalised."

Henry waved his hand in the air, suddenly desperate for this plan to go ahead and to deflect his council's suggestion of Katherine's marriage to himself.

For he did not care for the idea one bit.

"Tell Isabella de Castille and Ferdinand de Aragon that we accept their proposition, and that plans may commence to discuss the formalities."

Edmund Dudley, the king's President of the Council, nodded his head as he picked up his quill and began to take notes.

"Make sure Isabella and Ferdinand understand that they must pay Katherine's second half of the dowry before the marriage to Harry can take place. They have two and a half years before he is of age to marry, plenty of time to pay up. Only then will I allow this union to go ahead.

Katherine

He's dead.
He's dead.
He is really...dead.

Chapter 2

June 1503
Richmond Palace, Surrey

Prince Harry's older sister, Margaret Tudor, was sitting before her looking-glass, looking as sullen as on the day of her mother's funeral.
And she certainly felt as though someone had died, for her father was insisting that she marry the old King James IV of Scotland.
"I will speak to him," Margaret Beaufort, Princess Margaret's grandmother and namesake soothed as she brushed her granddaughter's hair lovingly, "You are too young to be married yet."
"My lord father will not listen," the princess replied, barely above a whisper, "he is desperate for alliances and to conclude the Treaty of Perpetual Peace with Scotland."
Margaret Beaufort sighed and then frowned, her forehead creasing between her eyebrows.
"The Tudor dynasty is not yet secure. Your brother and mother's deaths has rocked the foundation we have been building for decades. It is only natural that your father would wish to arrange good marriages for his remaining children. And this *is* a good match for you, Maggie. However, you are but thirteen, and I shall insist that the marriage should not take place until another year at least. I do not wish for you to endure what I did when I married your grandfather, Edmund Tudor."
Princess Margaret turned to face her grandmother, the matriarch of the Tudor family, and offered her a sad smile. She had heard the story many times, how a young Margaret Beaufort was married off – her *second* marriage – at just twelve-years-old to the twenty-four-year-old Edmund Tudor.

Her first marriage at nine-years-old had never been consummated due to hers and her husband's young ages, and her second marriage had not been expected to be consummated either for at least two years, when she would have been fourteen. But her new spouse had been eager to bed her, and young Margaret Beaufort had gone on to give birth to her only son, Henry Tudor, at just thirteen years old.

The trauma of the difficult birth on her young body had left the lady barren, as well as mentally scarred from the ordeal, and though she had married *twice* more since, she had never willingly lain with either of her other husbands.

Margaret Beaufort gently took her granddaughter's chin in her hand then and looked into her eyes.

"No girl should be made to marry before she is of age to conceive. I was thirteen when I birthed your father, and it nearly killed me. I will not allow such a thing to happen to you."

Though his mother had protested greatly against the union between the thirty-year-old Scottish king James IV to their thirteen-year-old Maggie, Henry Tudor paid his mother no heed.

"This alliance is too important," the king told his mother, desperate for her to understand, "The Treaty of Perpetual Peace between England and Scotland is of the utmost importance. We almost lost the alliance with Spain…England cannot afford to be without allies."

"Waiting another year for the girl to mature will not affect the treaty!" Margaret hissed at her son, wishing – not for the first time – that they had never been separated after her son's birth. For though he loved and respected his mother, Henry Tudor had grown up around men, and he could therefore never truly understand the terrifying life of a young girl of noble blood.

"It is done, mother!" the king said, his tone clipped.

There would be no more discussion.

July 1503

After some dispute over the Spanish Princess' dowry, England and Spain signed the finalised marriage treaty between Katherine of Aragon and the new Prince of Wales, Harry.
A small ceremony took place, followed by a banquet to commemorate the occasion.
It was clear to see that the twelve-year-old Prince Harry and the seventeen-year-old Princess Katherine enjoyed each other's company, many commenting on Harry's boisterous manner reaching new heights on that joyous day.
He had been – understandably – grief-stricken and sullen ever since his mother's death, and so to see him with a spark of life once again cheered the people of the court greatly.
Once the banquet was cleared, most of the courtiers headed to the dance floor and danced merrily, while others went off to the games tables in the back to play cards by the fire.
"Care for a game of chess, princess?" Harry called over the sound of the music and laughter of the court, craning his neck to be heard across the table.
Katherine smiled and nodded her head before rising from her seat at the high table.
Harry grinned and held out his arm to her, a chivalric display of affection which Katherine welcomed, and she giggled at her young betrothed.
They walked towards the stone chess table with their arms interlinked – the very image of a betrothed royal couple – and took their seats.
The pair played the game at leisure, enjoying the music all around them and sharing snippets of casual conversation that would set the foundation for many more to come, their likes

and dislikes, their favourite passages of the bible, their favourite hymns.

And even when, hours later, the princess wished to bid the court goodnight, Harry insisted they play just one more game of backgammon or cards, for it was proving to be a bright and warm day in the midst of too many dark and gloomy ones, and Harry wanted for it to never end.

Later that night, as Harry lay in bed exhausted from the day's celebrations, he considered his good fortune – to be betrothed to such a noble, gracious, and beautiful exotic princess.

But then a pang of guilt pierced through him, and the image of his dead brother flashed before his mind's eye.

He winced and scrunched his eyes shut at the memory, and in an effort to regain his previous joy, Harry forced his mind back to the day's contentment.

But then his thoughts wandered, and he replayed a day in which his brother had still been very much alive – the day when the beautiful *infanta* had wed Arthur.

At ten-years-old at the time, Harry had felt honoured to have been chosen to walk the Spanish princess down the aisle to her groom, and he remembered how giddy he felt at the sight of her in her wedding gown as the two of them stood outside St Paul's Cathedral before the ceremony had begun.

The sun had been shining brightly on that November morning, and he remembers thinking how radiant she had looked.

He had been nothing but happy for his older brother at the time of course, for back then Harry had still intended to pursue his chosen path of priesthood.

And yet he could remember that he had believed her to be the most beautiful creature on God's good Earth, even then.

But surely they had been no more than feelings of excitement for the day ahead. The festivities, the music, the food.

Regardless…it did not matter now.

For now, two years later, Harry was contracted to marry the exquisite Katherine himself.

Harry had believed it to have been a great honour to have walked the foreign princess down the aisle on that bright and sunny day.

But now, as he lay there pondering in the secluded hour of darkness, kept warm with giddiness and wine, it was rapidly beginning to feel more like fate.

"A papal dispensation will yet need to be issued," Margaret Beaufort said casually as she sat beside her son as they ate privately in the king's chambers.

"Of course," the king replied as he chewed.

"Whether Katherine and Arthur consummated or not is irrelevant," his mother continued absentmindedly, "The *infanta* was previously married to Harry's brother. And so, the Pope will need to console with God as to whether the former brother and sister in-law are permitted to marry."

"Yes, mother," Henry Tudor answered with a sigh of frustration as he picked up his cup of wine and sipped, wishing with all his heart that his wife was still here with him.

August 1503

Prince Harry stood beneath the stone archway with his younger sister, Mary, as they watched Maggie climb the steps of her carriage and fold herself into it, her long travel dress of maroon damask trailing behind her like a snake.

Mary, the youngest of Henry Tudor and Elizabeth of York's children, was crying audibly, her chin trembling as she sniffed every few seconds.

"Stop it," the young prince said under his breath as he continued to stare straight ahead and at the travel party that would follow Maggie up to Scotland.

Seven-year-old Mary ignored her older brother and continued to sob.

"Stop it, Mary," Harry said again, this time taking her little hand in his and squeezing it once.

He had meant to console her, but in his own sadness he had squeezed too tight, and Mary snatched her hand away and cried harder before turning and running away.

Harry watched her disappear into the darkness of the castle and sighed, then turned back to wave to his older sister.

He would likely never see Maggie again.

Just as he would never see his mother, or Arthur again.

But Maggie was not dead, at least.

Not yet, anyway, Prince Harry thought then, as the memory of his mother's lifeless face flashed before his eyes.

Harry sighed again and shook his head irritably; he mustn't think that way.

His mother's death in childbirth had been a tragedy, one that he would hopefully never experience again in his lifetime.

The guards called to each other then, once they had finally secured the travel trunks to the carriages and mounted their horses, ready for the long departure through England and into Scotland.

Maggie flashed her brother one last sad smile from the carriage window, which Harry returned as best as he could, though his chest was aching from all the loss he had experienced in this past year and a half.

As he stood and watched the hundreds of horses and men exiting the castle gates, Harry turned his mind to happier times in an effort to fight the melancholy.

He allowed the brighter thoughts to consume him as he turned and made his way inside.

A smile crept in as he slowly walked into the depths of the castle, his mind showing him the same images he had turned to more and more often of late in these seemingly never-ending times of gloom.

The sun shining golden on hair.
The enchanting chiming of a laugh.
The hint of a smile.
They were all images and memories of *her*.

November 1503

"Papal dispensation has been granted!" Henry VII proclaimed as he read the letter in his hand.
Margaret Beaufort clasped her wrinkled hands together, "Oh!" she breathed as she cast her eyes up and thanked God under her breath.
"It is good news, gentlemen!" Henry continued with a grin, "Arrangements may be made for the day that Harry comes of age!"
There was a mutter of relief and anticipation from among the Privy Council.
"Excellent news, Your Grace," one member of the council called out.
"Yes," Henry agreed as he passed the letter to his mother for her to peruse, "All is going to plan, and soon England and Spain will be united."
And Henry breathed a heavy sigh of relief, for there was suddenly hope that the Tudor House may yet be saved.

February 1504

The Tudor Dynasty was weak.
It had begun crumbling following the death of Prince Arthur and hadn't stopped crumbling since.
With the loss of his perfect son and heir, followed by that of his most beloved queen and their baby daughter, Henry had become more and more aware that the Tudors were not as valued as they had been without those that they had recently lost.

Henry had always known that the people of England had only accepted him as king all those years ago due to his promise to marry their Yorkist Flower – the princess Elizabeth of York – and thereby unifying the warring families of Lancaster and York. Their marriage had meant the end of the thirty-year Cousin's War, and that peace had been one of the main reasons why the people had accepted him as their king.

There had been some hiccups along the way of course – pretenders and rebellions; nothing unusual for a new king to deal with – but overall, he had been recognised as the true monarch by the people. And yet he had always known that any popularity he had, had come from who had been by his side to rule – the pure-blooded daughter of Edward IV, the White Flower to his Red.

Their first-born son, Arthur, had also been truly loved by the people, and he had shown great promise for the future.

He had been the perfect mix of Henry and Elizabeth...

But now the corner stones of his reign, his much-loved wife and heir, were gone and it was finally crystal clear to Henry that England tolerated their king, but they did not *like* their king.

Fair enough, he had been a paranoid and sneaky monarch at times, implementing new laws throughout the years that had allowed his spies to infiltrate noble people's households and interrogate chaplains and confessors so that Henry would always know if and when a new rebellion was taking shape, or another pretender was being moulded.

Of course, he had only ever put his spies to use if there had been cause for concern...Henry would not have even *needed* his spies at all if his people had simply remained *loyal* to him...

But he knew that those laws of disruption of privacy had not been the only thing to irk his people against him.

Henry had an insatiable need to keep the king's treasury bountiful.

His claim to the throne had been a feeble one...and it had always made him feel suspicious of anyone purer than he.

Because of this, he had developed a need to strengthen the crown and himself through the power of riches, and throughout the years it had become essential to quench his growing paranoia.

To accomplish these riches without engaging in wars, however, Henry had needed to bend the rules a little in his favour. And so, years prior, the king had employed Edmund Dudley.

Edmund Dudley had been no more than a lawyer at the time but had quickly attained the position of President of the King's Council through his loyalty to the king and his sharp intellect.

With Dudley's knowledge and connections in the legal system, the king had been able to introduce many taxes throughout the years to keep his noble people's monies diminished, while the king's own treasury reaped the benefits. The nobles, Henry knew, had all been too scared to confront their king about his actions for fear of reigniting the thirty-year war that his rise to power had ended.

But now that Henry VII was growing old and his much-beloved wife and son were gone, Henry knew the people would not continue in their acceptance of him and his antics for much longer. He knew he had aggravated the lords for far too long... and Harry was now the only hope he had left.

And if he wished to keep his dynasty from crumbling further, he would have to keep Harry safe from harm until he was ready to take over as king.

"Has Lord Burgavenny paid up yet?" Henry asked as he sipped his wine.

The President of the King's Council, Edmund Dudley sat beside Henry Tudor in the king's chambers, the two men sharing a pitcher of the finest wine as they went through the documents before them.

Edmund Dudley shook his head in response, "But he will," he said with a smirk as he passed a document to his king, "This arrived today," he said, his heavy-lidded eyes suggesting boredom, though Henry knew Dudley to be very astute.

Henry took the document and perused its contents while Edmund spoke, "The nobles are, of course, disgruntled at our new increase of bonds, my lord. But we knew they would be."

Henry nodded as he continued looking down at the document.

"Though I agreed – and still do – with your highness' need to clamp down on the nobles, I fear it is not enough," Dudley continued with an exaggerated sigh, "There is always the possibility of civil unrest. Especially now."

Henry nodded again, "I am aware of this," he replied monotonously before flicking the document back to Dudley with a heavy sigh, "I have been considering the fragility of my lineage of late," Henry admitted then.

Edmund Dudley nodded, hardly surprised by the remark, for it was obvious that this would be on the old king's mind.

"I'm considering hiding Harry away for a while," Henry continued, looking sideways at his trusted advisor.

Dudley squinted his heavy-lidded eyes, "To keep him hidden from what?"

Henry raked his fingers through his greying hair, "From harm, mostly," he admitted, "I wish to increase his education of course, to continue his learning of how to rule without the distractions of fun."

"Ah," Dudley replied, "yes. Fun can be dangerous, especially in your highness' situation."

"Precisely. He is my only remaining hope at continuing what I began."

"So…how much *fun* is to cease for the boy?" Dudley asked, picking up his quill.

Henry pursed his lips and narrowed his eyes in thought. Then he shrugged and raked his long fingers through his hair once again.

Dudley intertwined his fingers together and leaned forward, "If I might be so bold, my lord…you cannot be too careful."

Henry raised his eyebrows, "Jousting certainly has to stop."

Dudley nodded, "Certainly. Though if you are to disallow jousting but not riding in general, the risk is not much lessened."

The king sighed once again, this time in frustration, and Dudley, sensing a long and tedious afternoon, seized an opportunity for simplicity.

"To easy your mind, my lord… why not simply disallow all of it?"

Katherine

The grief has consumed me.
And I allow it.
I welcome the pain, for what meaning does my life now have without him in it?
Who even am I now?
Without him...how am I meant to go on?

Chapter 3

April 1504
Durham House, London

Princess Katherine of Aragon had been granted Durham House since the sudden death of her first husband, Arthur Tudor, two years prior.

She and her household had been allowed to reside there for her year of mourning and during the in-between stage of her life that had followed, where she had been hovering in limbo amid her marriages to the two Princes of England.

But God was watching over her, she knew, for though tragedy had struck her late young husband, she had come out of that nightmare unscathed.

She still did not know why God had seen fit to spare her from the sweating sickness she and Arthur had both contracted. And throughout the many months of solitude, she would often find herself wondering, *why spare me and not him?*

Since that tragedy she had prayed for answers, answers to the many mysteries of life and death.

Was she *really* meant to become Queen of England?

All her young life she had been told she would be, had been brought up to become the wife of Arthur Tudor – but his death had rocked her faith in her supposed destiny.

And since then, she had spent many months feeling guilty for having survived when Arthur had not.

Her mother's voice would echo in her mind in those moments of guilt, whispers of how God had not been ready to call her to Him because her destiny as Queen of England was not yet achieved.

And then her betrothal to Prince Harry had been suggested by her parents and swiftly accepted by her former – and future –

father-in-law, and her belief in her destiny as Queen of England had returned to her.

Not only had all parties been consenting to this turn of events, but the Pope, too, had recently allowed the union, and it was with that final detail that Katherine believed that she *was* on God's chosen path.

Nothing could stop it now.

And as soon as Harry turned fourteen next year on the 28th of June 1505, she – the Princess of Spain and daughter to the mighty Isabella de Castille and Ferdinand de Aragon – would be heading towards her future as Queen of England once more.

All she would have to do now was wait.

But her stomach lurched then at the thought of heading down the aisle once again, worry for the unknown twisting her stomach into knots.

But she suppressed her fear.

Nothing but good things were henceforth to come her way, Katherine was sure of it.

For indeed, one tragedy had already struck the young princess in regard to wedded bliss.

Surely this next time, all would be well.

May 1504
Richmond Palace, Surrey

Prince Harry pulled the bowstring back tightly before letting loose his arrow, only for it to hit the bottom corner of the straw target.

The few observing young courtiers chuckled amicably, a couple of them clapping in playful mockery, but Harry only laughed.

"It was better," one of the young men said in the prince's defence, "Next time concentrate on your breathing."

The young man's name was Charles Brandon, and he was one of Prince Harry's closest friends.

Charles was the only surviving son of Sir William Brandon, who had been King Henry VII's standard-bearer at the Battle of Bosworth in 1485, when Harry's father had defeated Richard III and claimed the throne of England for himself.

Sir William Brandon, Charles' father, had died during that very battle, and England's new King Henry VII, acknowledging William Brandon's loyalty, chose to repay this debt by having his son, Charles, brought up in his court.

Charles had been just two years older than Henry VII's own eldest son, Arthur, but they had never bonded quite so well as he had done with his younger son, Harry, though he was seven years his senior.

But since Arthur's death, Harry and Charles had become very close, the young prince confiding in his friend above anyone else about his troubles.

It was Charles' turn to take his shot next, and Harry stepped aside to observe the young man's form.

Charles – at twenty-years-old and therefore having had more practice – hit the mark dead-centre, which was met with cheering from the others.

"An excellent shot, Charles," Harry's younger sister, the little Princess Mary called from among the small crowd as she clapped excitedly.

Charles bowed theatrically in the princess' direction.

Harry stepped forward, "My turn –"

But the prince was interrupted by the arrival of a messenger then, who had come over the field at a brisk pace.

"Pardon the intrusion, Your Grace, but the king requests your urgent presence," the messenger said, "He is in the council chambers."

Harry handed his bow to one of the other boys and began to follow the messenger.

"Shall I come with you, Harry?" Charles called from behind him.

Thirteen-year-old Harry turned and continued walking away from the archery stand backwards, "No need, Charles," he called with a grin, "No doubt I shall return soon."

"You are to cease all dangerous and childish activities, Your Grace," Edmund Dudley proclaimed nonchalantly as he stood beside the king in the council chambers, who was busy signing documents before him.

Harry narrowed his eyes at his father's advisor. He didn't like how Edmund Dudley spoke for the king. Surely his father could tell him this himself.

"What activities might those be?" Harry asked, since he did not partake in anything especially different to any other boy his age.

But then again, Harry was no longer just like any other boy his age.

Dudley opened his mouth to speak but the king beat him to it.

"Archery," King Henry replied without looking up from his paperwork, "Horse riding, hunting, jousting. There will be no more of it."

Prince Harry was struck utterly mute, his father's announcement surprising the young prince.

In his silence, King Henry looked up at Dudley and, showing him one of the documents, mumbled a question at him. Dudley listened and then replied in the same quiet whispers.

The aloof interaction taking place before him as though he were not even present infuriated Harry, and he stood flabbergasted before the two men.

The king returned his attention to his son and expelled an exasperated sigh, knowing the boy would want an explanation.

"I cannot risk you, Harry," he stated, "You are England's future. Its *only* future."

Harry nodded, standing a little straighter at the remark, though the pressure of it all weighing on him. He glanced over at Dudley, who stared back at the young prince with a smug smile on his lips.

Harry wanted to reach over and swipe the smile right off his face, but of course he did not. Instead, he turned his attention back to his king.

"Might I return to the archery field to observe at least?" the prince asked, grasping at straws for the sake of avoiding utter boredom.

The king looked over at Dudley for the briefest of moments, but it was enough for Harry to realise who was really responsible for the tightening on the rack of this excruciating torture.

Dudley's mouth twitched slightly in response to his king's look and Henry returned his gaze to Harry before shaking his head.

"No, son," he said, "Your safety is of the utmost importance."

Harry scoffed a perplexed laugh, looking from one boring old man to the other, "But father –"

"Harry!" the king interrupted sternly then, meeting his son's gloomy stare, "You shall remain out of trouble until I say otherwise. I have arranged for more education to fill your days so that you will not have time to resent me."

Too late for that, Harry thought, his pale cheeks glowing red with disappointment.

His father continued, "We have little time left to whip you into shape to inherit my throne. And I cannot rely on hope alone that nothing shall happen to you in that time."

His father need say no more, for deep down Harry understood the reasoning behind the decision to seclude the young boy from all matters of fun.

And yet, his understanding did little to lessen the hatred Harry felt towards his father and his lackey in that moment.

August 1504

The Spanish Princess had been taken ill.
Throughout the months of Summer, Katherine had been confined to her bed, chills and fevers overcoming her frequently, and word soon spread that she was unlikely to survive.
"No, she cannot die!" Harry exclaimed when his grandmother, Margaret Beaufort, brought him the news of his betrothed's condition.
Though Harry had not seen much of his intended over the past year, he maintained that same ardent admiration and regard for her as he had done since their formal betrothal.
In his mind, the image of her burned brightly: an exotic Madonna with the purest, noblest blood running through her veins.
But his admiration had evolved into something else in the more recent months of adolescence, where he had begun to envision her in his private moments – the golden glimmer of her hair in sunlight never failing to evoke a shiver of excitement in him.
To Harry, no other could compete with Katherine of Aragon. Not only was she a pure princess of the blood, but her beauty reigned supreme to the young prince. Her youth and plump figure promised fertility, and her royal upbringing promised aristocratic wisdom.
She was the *perfect* bride for him, for she would be able to fill the gaps in the knowledge he knew he lacked in terms of how to rule a kingdom.
He *needed* her. She must not die!
"The physicians have observed her," Margaret Beaufort explained carefully, for fear of upsetting the prince further, "and they do not seem to be able to find the cause for her ailment. It is a mystery as to what is wrong with her."

Harry shook his head, bewildered, but he did not reply.

He darted his eyes all around the room, his mind frantically searching for anything that would aid his betrothed. But there was nothing he could do.

"Lady Grandmother," Harry mumbled tearfully, like the young boy that he was, "I do not wish for her to die."

Margaret *tutted* in sympathy and opened her arms for him to step into, "She is strong," she cooed as she stroked Harry's coppery head like a child, though he was already taller than her, "She may yet overcome this. Physicians do not know everything."

Harry lifted his head from her shoulder and forced a smile, suddenly embarrassed by his display of emotions.

Margaret, sensing the boy's discomfort, squeezed his shoulders, "There's only one thing we can do that will aid her."

Harry's eyes widened briefly with hope and curiosity.

Margaret smiled at her favourite grandchild, "We must pray."

Harry did pray.

He prayed ardently each night for Katherine's recovery.

But in the light of day, as reports continued to arrive of the princess' continued ill health, Harry considered that perhaps praying would not be enough, and he decided that he would write to his beloved in the hope that his proclamation of adoration would aid her towards healing.

In his seclusion from outdoor activities, Harry spent many hours composing cheerful poems for his lady, some about his admiration of her, others of the day that they would be wed.

He sent each of them off to Durham House with a sense of pride that he was giving Katherine something to hold onto during these long months of illness, something joyful to bring light to her gloom.

And then, when news of her slow recuperation began to suddenly arrive, Harry took great delight in the belief that his chivalric poetry had likely been the cure to saving her.

November 1504

Katherine of Aragon had fully recovered.
The illness had faded as mysteriously as it had appeared, and Margaret Beaufort gave thanks to God for sparing Harry's bride.
However, one tragedy seemed to birth another, for only weeks after reports of the princess' recuperation had arrived, disastrous news from Spain shook the English court.
"The death of Isabella de Castille has torn Spain apart," one of Henry Tudor's advisors said as they sat around the council table, the roaring fire warming their backs, "the regions of Castille and Aragon are no longer united under one co-ruling king and queen, and Spain is likely to descend into civil unrest."
Margaret Beaufort looked to her son to assess his thoughts as only a mother could.
He was rubbing at his beardless chin, his eyes cast down at the wooden table, focused on nothing as he considered this new outcome.
With this turn of events, Spain was suddenly weak.
When the alliance between England and Spain had been arranged through Arthur's union to Katherine many years ago, Spain had been a force to be reckoned with. Ruled by the two reigning monarchs of each Christian region of the country, Spain had been an incredible ally at the time.
But with the queen of Castille suddenly dead and her land inherited by her eldest daughter, Juana, Spain was now a country torn in two, the regions no longer united by marriage.
"We could arrange for a better match for Harry…" the king said absentmindedly as he continued to think, "Ferdinand

continues to refuse to send the *infanta's* dowry anyway. And without her dowry, signed treaty or not, the marriage cannot go ahead."

The men at the council table nodded their heads.

"A betrothal to another princess would see to a dowry paid in full," one councilman said, "Ferdinand has always been a snake!"

Margaret watched from her seat at the table as her son mulled over the new information, unsure of how she felt about this potential new outcome for her Harry.

She had noticed that the prince had retreated into himself since his brother's and mother's deaths, his formerly lively and playful personality having been chipped away by the sudden responsibility that lay before him – as well as his father's decision to seclude him from most activities and festivities, in an effort to keep him safe.

His betrothal to the Spanish princess had been the only thing to bring a glimmer of light back into his eyes – even if just momentarily. Margaret had noticed it like the fragile flickering of a candle in the wind.

Harry may not have wanted his brother's *crown*, but he wanted his brother's *widow*.

"Surely the small matter of an inconclusive dowry should not stand in the way of this alliance," Margaret added then as her thoughts of a happy Harry teased at the corners of her mind, "to break the betrothal now could lead to unrest closer to home, Your Grace."

She hoped to convey her meaning to her son without having to utter the words, for she knew that none of the king's councilmen cared for the young prince's preference of bride. But she hoped that his father would.

May 1505

As king, Henry VII could not simply choose his son's happiness above the wellbeing of the entire kingdom. And the promise of financial gain through a dowry paid in full by another nation, was too important to pass up.

"Send for my son," the king said to his groom one afternoon, who bowed briefly and scurried away.

With Harry's fifteenth birthday fast approaching, time to come to a conclusion was running out and Henry Tudor needed to free Harry from his betrothal if he wished to consider better brides for his heir.

Henry would have to break his decision to his son. A decision he knew Harry would not take well, for the boy had developed feelings for the Spanish *infanta*.

The young pair had not had many moments together, Henry thought absently as he awaited the arrival of his son, though it seemed Harry had become smitten with the older princess. Her beauty was, no doubt, a factor – and he couldn't even blame his son, for he too could remember being young and enchanted by the beauty of women.

But the future of England was at stake. And Harry's happiness did not outweigh England's need for financial expansion; for currency, Henry Tudor believed, was what lay at the core of a king's success.

"The Prince of Wales, Your Grace," the king's groom announced as he returned with the young man in tow.

"Father," Harry said in greeting, his voice deeper than the last time they had spoken, which Henry could not even recall when that might have been.

The king waved his son over to the fire and the boy did as he was ordered, though Henry noticed a tension in Harry's jawline as he approached.

There was resentment in his eyes towards his father.

Henry smiled sadly to himself; Harry was becoming a man.

"You wished to see me, father," Harry said, his tone suggesting he wanted to speed the meeting along.

The king smiled up at his son and blinked slowly. He would not be pushed to hurry up. Not by Harry, or by anyone.

Harry might have suddenly and tragically become his father's heir…but by God, Henry Tudor was still the king!

"Take a seat, Harry," Henry offered, jerking his chin at the chair before him.

Harry looked at the seat, then back at his father, the tension between them palpable, "I'll stand if it's all the same to you."

Henry shrugged as though he did not care, but the snub was duly noted, and though he had planned to soften the news he had to share with his son, Henry now decided he had to reestablish who was in charge here.

"You are to revoke your betrothal to the Spanish *infanta*."

Stunned, Harry stared back at his father, unsure of how to respond.

"Spain is no longer a viable option for a strong alliance," Henry explained in his son's silence, "And Ferdinand de Aragon refuses to send his daughter's full dowry. England needs a stronger and more financially practical alliance."

Harry swallowed before nodding his head, though his eyebrows remained bunched together in confusion.

"What other lady is to be Katherine's replacement?" he managed to ask, though he did not care for anyone else to be his wife.

King Henry shifted in his seat, "There is no other concrete alternative yet. But by breaking your formal betrothal, it will open new options."

"And England *needs* these…new options?" Harry asked, not fully convinced of his father's reasoning.

Henry rose from his seat and licked his lips. He walked over to his son and placed a firm hand on his shoulder, "You have a responsibility to the country, my boy. A strong alliance must always come before your own heart's desires. There will be other princesses."

Harry nodded slowly as he maintained his father's sharp eye contact.

He could see in the king's eyes that he was serious – he really did wish to rid himself of the Spanish alliance, despite how fruitful it had been just a short while ago.

Harry's mind was racing, suddenly tragically confused as to what he ought to do, his duty and his heart battling for the upper hand in his conscience.

England must be in desperate need of monies…it's economic development must be at a decline…England must *need* for Harry to do the right thing to financially support it…

What other reason could there possibly be for his father to so easily throw away his only son's happiness?

27th June 1505
Durham House, London

It was the eve before Katherine of Aragon's wedding – for the second time – to the Prince of Wales.

Tomorrow she would be wed yet again, but she was no longer anxious like before, for she had put her faith in God that this time was meant to last.

"A visitor, my lady," her lady-in-waiting's voice suddenly cut through the silence of her bedchambers.

Katherine's smooth, pale forehead twitched into a frown, "At this hour?" and she looked out of the window and into the darkness, as if to prove her point.

Her dark-skinned lady only shrugged before the doors to her bedchambers were abruptly opened and Prince Harry entered the room.

Katherine rose from her seat by the fire, taken aback by the unannounced intrusion. But she did not show it, for a royal princess must always present composure, no matter the circumstances – that had been one of her first lessons as a royal daughter of Spain.

As the princess looked upon her future husband – copper-haired, blue-eyed, and with an aura that exuded confidence – she realised that Prince Harry had grown more handsome since the last time they had seen each other.

Though he did have a weak chin, Katherine had noticed. A chin which he had inherited from his mother.

Over the years, Katherine had sometimes forgotten that he was younger than her by six years, for he had always carried himself with poise and wrote of love with such fervour, that it was easy to forget he was but on the verge of young adulthood.

But she noticed now that – for a reason yet unbeknownst to Katherine – he was not exuding that same poise tonight.

"Your Grace," Katherine said in greeting as she curtsied, suddenly wishing she hadn't dressed for comfort in her garb of wool but chosen a finer dress of silk or velvet instead.

If she had had some forewarning, she would have changed.

But Harry did not seem to notice.

The young prince bowed his head at her quickly in reply, and when their eyes met from across the room, Harry's neck blotched red.

Katherine, believing his reaction to be due to nerves, smiled slightly to think him so besotted with her, which – though she did not yet return his feelings – was certainly something she appreciated in the man she would be joined to spend her life with.

"I have come to –" Harry said before stopping short, his voice catching in his throat, the words he had been instructed to say choking him from within.

Katherine cocked her head to one side, her hands clasped before her in an elegant and regal stance as she waited patiently.

Harry couldn't help but admire her.

Her elegance and sovereignty drew him to her like a moth to a flame. And it made what he had to do so much harder.

He cleared his throat and swallowed.

"I have come to repudiate our betrothal, much as it pains me to do so."

Katherine stood frozen, her eyes fixed on Harry's in shock.

They stared at one another, Katherine's lady feeling suddenly extremely aware of her own presence during this uncomfortable moment, and she took a step backwards into the shadows.

The fire in the hearth cracked then before sending a gust of sparks up into the chimney, and the heavy silence was broken.

"On the eve of our wedding…?" Katherine finally breathed, her horror beginning to ebb into disbelief.

Harry only hung his head, no longer able to meet her gaze as the misery consumed him, but he was glad she would not see the forlorn tremble of his chin.

"I am come to inform you that I only accepted the terms of our betrothal because my father and king had wished for it, at the time. But now he wishes for me to renege it. And I must do what my lord father expects of me."

The lie cut like shards of glass in Harry's throat, and he was glad to have broken eye contact with the object of his affection, for he could not bear to see the hurt in her eyes at his words of rejection.

Because in truth, Harry had happily accepted the terms of their betrothal. It had been the only thing to have brought him joy after his brother's and mother's deaths, Maggie's departure to Scotland, baby Catherine's death…

Not only did Katherine set alight a flame in his belly, but Harry believed her to be the epitome of royalty.

She had been educated as well as any prince of Europe by her noble parents, and she had the tactful, gracious charm of royalty trained from birth.

But as Henry VII's only surviving heir, Harry must do as he was told if his father believed it to be in the country's best interest.

There will be other princesses, his father's words resounded in his ears then.

And though Harry had reluctantly agreed to do what was asked of him, he had stormed out of the king's chambers earlier that day, expressing his heartache in the only way he knew how, *There are none like this one.*

"It is my father's doing," Katherine mumbled the following day as she awoke on what should have been her wedding day, "He fails to send the rest of my dowry."

"I will fetch the ink and parchment," her lady, Catalina, said as she stood up from Katherine's bed.

They had not yet dressed, the two young women having chosen to evaluate yesterday's occurrences with a fresh mindset and a clear head first thing in the morning.

And they had concluded that ulterior motives must be at work here.

"The way he looked at you last night," Catalina said as she walked over to the writing desk by the window, her Spanish accent strong, "He wanted to marry you today. This is not his decision."

"No," Katherine agreed sullenly, and Harry's poems and letters of ardent adoration sent to her while she lay dying the year before replayed in her mind.

Catalina returned with the parchment and quill and handed them to the princess.

"We shall spend the day abed drafting your letter to your father," her lady said, her dark eyes shining with determination to fix this terrible situation for her mistress, "And tonight we send it off with the fastest messenger in all of England."

January 1506

Katherine's father, Ferdinand de Aragon, ignored his daughter's letters, and for the many months that followed, Katherine was *persona non grata* within the English court.
With her father continuing to refuse to pay the remainder of her dowry, Henry VII no longer felt obligated to financially support her.
And without the continuation of his charitable income, Katherine was no longer able to pay many of her servants.
She was living in limbo.
In the first few months, Katherine would wake each morning with the hope that this would be the day that her father would see reason and fulfil his duty to her as his daughter. But as each day turned into night, the hope she had started off with would slip away and before she knew it, seven months had passed without a word from her father in regard to her future.
To find herself living in a country where one was suddenly looked upon as a pariah, but having nowhere to return to, or even to call home; knowing that with her mother's death, Katherine was suddenly worthless to both of the countries she had grown up belonging to…it was a painful realisation.
And then one day she awoke to find many of her household had abandoned her in the night, many of her servants and ladies having left to seek employment elsewhere – somewhere they would receive a reward for their labour.
Katherine couldn't even begrudge them, for if she too had other options she might have pursued them.
But alas, she had been born with a destiny and sent to England with a goal, and the only thing on the cards for her was to one day become Queen of England.
But as time had gone on, the luxuries she had been used to as a princess had quickly begun to fade, and Katherine had needed to resort to selling her jewels and tapestries to make ends meet. And if the maltreatment were to continue for much

longer, basic necessities such as food or wood for the fires, would too become a thing of the past.

"We will sell the plates next," Katherine told her Moorish lady, one of the only remaining familiar faces from her homeland, "It will see us through the next few weeks."

"My lady, you must eat," Catalina fussed as Katherine continued to walk hastily through the cold stone corridors of Durham House, her haste being fuelled partly by the need to stay warm, and partly by anger.

Katherine's formally full figure had melted away in recent months, lack of nutrition as well as stress having eaten away at her womanly shape.

"I shall eat once my household has a full belly," the princess replied as her empty stomach tightened at the prospect of many days of sustaining themselves on nothing more than prayer.

"My belly is full, Your Grace," Catalina lied as they entered Katherine's bedchamber, and she spotted a plate on the wooden table. One of the few remaining servants must have brought up a plate of supper while they had been out.

Catalina walked over to the table and picked up one of the hard crusts of bread, the contrast of the peasant's food upon the plate of gold too ironic to bear.

"Here, my lady," she said as she held the bread out for Katherine to take, "I do not want it."

Katherine took the crust sheepishly and sniffed it before nibbling at it cautiously. She did not know how long this piece of hard bread would have to last her until her next meal, but even for her to eat it instead of her lady made Katherine feel sick to her stomach.

It was her daily conundrum of recent months – whether she ate the crust of bread or not – for the nausea brought on by this entire series of events was unavoidable.

Her life was in the hands of two stubborn men.

Two men fighting over riches that should be hers by right.

Riches neither of *them* truly needed. And they certainly didn't need it as much as she, who was quite literally wasting away due to their greed.

But she was no more than a mere woman, and women did not have a say in this world of men.

She would continue hanging in pendulum in this man's world, wondering whether this crusty piece of bread would be hers or her lady's final meal before death caught up to them.

She stuffed the remainder of the bread into her mouth and chewed it angrily then as she shook her head.

They could not go on like this.

Something would have to give!

Katherine

His eyes still haunt me.
His beautiful, pale blue eyes.
I will never forget them, no matter how many years might pass.
We had not been granted much time together.
But the few moments we shared have been etched into my heart – miniature portraits, snapshots in time.
I will never forget that first boy.
That first boy that had had so much promise.

Chapter 4

September 1506
Richmond Palace, Surrey

"The princess is starving," Margaret Beaufort told her son the king, though she was aware that he already knew, "she suffers often from fevers and chills and is said to be very weak."

"The princess *chooses* not to eat," one member of the king's council said, to whom Margaret directed a sharp look in response and the man shrunk back into his seat.

"It is true, mother," the king said in his advisor's defence, but he knew it was meagre, "She is extremely pious, much like yourself."

"And yet, here I am, looking much healthier than that poor girl," Margaret replied, but Henry ignored her.

"Ferdinand de Aragon has sent a letter promising the full payment of the *infanta's* dowry by March of next year," the king declared then, as though to suggest the princess need only hold on until then, "If he stays true to his promise we shall reconsider where we stand with him. But Prince Harry is still free to marry another. Until the dowry is paid, Harry is not tied to Katherine. And negotiations are being made to betroth him to Eleanor de Castille, to make a treaty with the new Queen of Castille, Juana, instead."

"Would Ferdinand hear of this?" an advisor asked, wondering whether it was a secret arrangement, or a tactical one, to put pressure on Ferdinand to pay up.

Henry Tudor shrugged, "I would imagine he will, since he is Juana de Castille's father."

"Pitting the newly separated regions of Spain against one another with this, and using Harry as the bargaining chip, will not bring you the peace you seek to gain with this treaty,

Henry," Margaret Beaufort said then as she leaned forward in her seat, trying to keep her tone from sounding too much like a mother scolding her child.

Her son shrugged, as if he did not care either way, but there was no fooling his mother, who looked up at him with narrowed eyes.

And as the council meeting continued, Margaret was left wondering if Henry had really gone through all of this only to beat Ferdinand at his own stubborn game.

June 1507
Durham House

Ferdinand did not pay the rest of Katherine's dowry by March, and before long another year had passed with little improvement to Katherine of Aragon's dire circumstances – a year in which Spain and England's relationship continued to deteriorate, politics and greed being at the very heart of every disagreement.

And then, much to everyone's confusion, King Ferdinand recalled his imperial ambassador back to Spain with the intention of assigning another in his stead.

"He has appointed *me* his new ambassador," Katherine said after reading her father's letter, which she knew Henry VII must have received a copy of.

Catalina stared at her mistress, "You?" she replied, her dark eyes wide in her sunken sockets, "But women are not ambassadors, are they?"

Katherine shook her head, stunned, "There has never been a woman ambassador in all of European history," she confirmed.

Catalina blinked slowly, speechless at this new development for her mistress and for her, for this surely meant Katherine would be receiving some kind of income.

It seemed they would not be left to starve after all.

"Your father has saved us," Catalina breathed.

But Katherine did not thank her father for this gift, for she knew he was nothing if not tactful, and he had certainly not done this for her. His ability to leave his own daughter to fend for herself had taught her that her father cared little for her wellbeing unless he got something in return for it.

No, God was who was behind this turn of events. For though it did indeed mean that they would not succumb to starvation, this position meant so much more to Katherine than a pitiful income. This position granted her a place among the English court – a position which would see to it that she would be respected.

She would no longer continue to be shunned and kept out the way in Durham House.

This was her ticket in – her chance to show King Henry and his advisors just how educated and capable she had been brought up to be.

As imperial ambassador – the *first* female ambassador in European history – Katherine would showcase her knowledge of politics, language, and negotiation, and the English court will be amazed.

Yes, this was the turning point for Katherine of Aragon, she could feel it in her bones.

And this surely meant that the worst was finally behind her.

September 1507
Richmond Palace, Surrey

King Henry's health was failing, and the people of England were beginning to look to the future.

There was suddenly much talk among the civilians and noble folk alike, whispers of Prince Harry's suspicious seclusion away from the public eye, and rumours had soon begun to spread that perhaps he was not as prepared as he ought to be to take over when their old king were to die.

"We need to bring Harry back to court," the king told his mother as he sat by the roaring fire, wrapped in furs.

Margaret Beaufort nodded at her son's decision and gently placed the back of her hand on his clammy forehead.

"I shall arrange it, Henry," she said with a forced smile, hoping to take some pressure off him so that he may recover. Henry nodded in thanks, "Harry is a good lad," he mumbled, "I need to show him off to the court. The people will warm to him."

Margaret agreed.

Though she loved her son more than any other, Margaret was well aware of the people's growing discontent towards their king.

His heavy taxations and desperate need to dampen the noble's control over their own households had aggravated too many to name, and in this hour of weakness, Henry Tudor had to make sure to remind England that the one who was to follow him would bring with him a breath of fresh air.

Harry, now a handsome teenager, was loved by many, his laidback charm and boisterous character having always been easy to love.

Stowing him away had been the right thing to do for a time, yes – his safety and kingly education had been of the utmost importance – but now priorities were shifting, and with Henry's health failing him, the Tudors would have to play their cards right.

"Let Harry arrange the Spring Tournament," the king said before coughing into his closed fist, "But he must not partake in the jousting!"

Margaret leaned forward and patted her son's arm, "*Shhh,*" she soothed, "Do not trouble your mind with this, my son. Mother will take care of everything."

November 1507

Four years had passed since Harry's father had ordered he be stowed away for his own safety.
Four years of watching from windows as the court partook in jousts and archery tournaments while he remained secluded in his chambers.
But worse than even that had been the many months he and his small household had spent hidden away in separate residences to the court, where he had spent day after day with his nose in a textbook or being lectured by boring old men about boring old things.
But upon his restoration to court, he was met with much delight from his friends and courtiers, all of them glad to see their prince's return as though he had been away at war, when he had in fact been upstairs in his quarters or residing at a nearby residence.
Harry had grown into a handsome and brilliant young man, and his tutors had been gushing for months of his great understanding of history, philosophy, Greek and music.
He wasn't Arthur. But he would have to do…
It was finally time for the king to show off his heir to his increasingly frustrated people.

March 1508

The Spring Tournament, organised by Prince Harry, was a spectacular event which lasted for days, and at its centre was the chivalric armoured knights, jousting on horseback.
Prince Harry however, though he had proved himself a brilliant jouster in his younger years, continued prohibited from taking part, his father continuing too fearful to risk his only heir.

And yet Harry enjoyed his taste of freedom nonetheless, and watching the tournaments among the other nobles gave him much cause for happiness.

"I cannot wait to get involved once more," Henry admitted to his friend, Charles Brandon, as they observed the jousters. Charles was now a young man of twenty-three with a mop of wavy dark brown hair on his head and smile that made all the ladies swoon, though he had recently married Anne Browne in a secret ceremony.

"Soon, no doubt," Charles mumbled in return, casting a sideways glance at Harry beside him and raising his eyebrows meaningfully.

"He continues unwell then," Harry muttered quietly as he watched the jousters barrel towards each other.

Charles shrugged and the crowd around them burst into cheers as one jouster was dismounted by his opponent's blow. Harry clapped and laughed heartily, "Ah I love it!" he exclaimed excitedly.

"Harry…" the king called sternly over to his son from his throne some rows back, making his disapproval of his son's excitement for such violence known.

Throughout the event, the people of the observing crowd – many of which were nobles and lords – had noticed the young prince's enthusiasm for the sport – a sport which valued chivalry, honour, and glory. And many began to mutter beneath their breaths just how different the young prince appeared to be to his overbearing and calculating father.

As the tournament continued throughout the afternoon, followed by a banquet, music and dancing, Harry mingled among the crowd through all of it, talking openly with lords and ambassadors, and dancing with several ladies.

His charm was noted by many. His charisma was appreciated by most.

And though King Henry was not yet aware of it, a shift in allegiance had this day begun.

At the end of the evening, while Henry watched from his throne as Harry swiftly exited the great hall with a young lady in tow, grinning boyishly from ear to ear, the old king nodded in saddened understanding: his reign was coming to an end.

April 1508

When Harry had been requested to return to court life six months prior, his father had been secretive about the whys and wherefores of it.
But at the age of sixteen, Harry had not stopped to ask why he was suddenly allowed some semblance of freedom once more, and he had instead taken the gift and run with it.
And in those last six months, Harry had certainly made up for lost time.
Upon tasting liberty, Harry had discovered many new things his younger self had not had the chance to previously experience, gambling being one of the thrilling new activities he so enjoyed of late.
It had been a delightful new discovery, the thrill of the game igniting a spark in the boy's chest, even on the occasions where he faced a loss.
But above even that had been the thrill of the discovery of women.
Since his return to court, the young prince had received much attention from the fairer sex, and in the months that had followed, he had bedded several ladies of the court.
The ladies had been of all shapes, sizes, hair colour, and rank. Some beautiful, some experienced, some shy, some even utterly hideous.
And yet…none had managed to erase the image in his mind that had been torturing him for the past three years: the image of Katherine of Aragon's face when he had broken off their engagement.

And now, Prince Harry was unsure of what to do, for he was torn between his strong sense of duty and his even stronger will.

"I had been confined to the life of a scholar," Harry complained to his close friend Charles Brandon one afternoon as they walked the palace gardens.

"I hardly ever left the boundaries of my chambers, as you know," Harry continued.

Charles nodded, "Yes, I received all your letters."

Harry sighed then, "It was all Dudley's doing," he mumbled spitefully, though he held contempt for both Dudley and his father alike.

Charles shrugged, "The king wished to mould you into the best version of yourself so that you would be ready to rule England when the time comes. He only did what he believed to be right for the country's future, and yours."

Harry frowned and kicked at a loose stone on the path before them, "I know all that," he said, "And though I enjoyed learning for the most part, I am painfully aware that –" he looked over his shoulder then in case anyone would be listening, though they remained alone, "this is not what I was born to do."

Charles offered his friend a tight-lipped smile at the confession but gave no response.

Harry continued.

"Arthur had loved *every* part of this kingly education, even the mundane ones of taxation, politics, and oration."

Charles grimaced at that.

"But I feel like I was built for other things," the prince continued, "*Nothing* gives me more joy than hunting, riding, or discussions of past wars," he listed them off on his fingers, "Especially of Henry V's glory against France…"

The two young men shared a look of admiration for the past King of England and his achievements then, before falling silent for a moment.

Charles hung his head in the stillness, allowing the young prince to sift through his thoughts.

"I have known for years that my father hoped to turn me into something I'm not," he admitted, "But it only recently dawned on me that what my father wished to mould me into… was Arthur himself."

Charles inhaled slowly, his eyebrows raised as he considered whether he should reply at all, for it was a sensitive subject.

But Harry went on as he looked up into the distance and squinted his eyes at the orange sunset, "I will never be like Arthur," he mumbled pensively, "I have too much lust for life to be entertained by the gentle lull of a book, or the careful perusing of a treaty."

Charles breathed a small laugh, for he knew that to be very true indeed.

Though he hadn't known Arthur long, Charles had immediately noticed upon his admittance at court that the two Tudor princes had been complete opposites, and though Arthur had died before he had reached an age to truly find himself, Charles had thought that he hadn't appeared to be the kind of boy who would have been interested in the forms of entertainment that he and Harry enjoyed so much. Which was why Charles had bonded with the younger of the two princes, despite having been closer in age to Arthur.

For like Charles, Harry was full of life.

The prince sighed irritably all of a sudden then, "I don't know what to do, Charles," he said.

Charles looked at his friend, unsure of what he meant, "In regard to what, Harry?"

Harry bent over and picked up a pebble, began tossing it lazily up into the air and letting it plop back into his open palm.

"Katherine," he replied with a sheepish, downcast glance.

Charles smiled and nodded slowly as he looked at his prince, "Ah," he mumbled knowingly, "your sweet lady love."

Harry breathed an embarrassed laugh.

"Have all the others not been enough to erase her from your mind?" the older boy asked impishly.

Harry shook his head, then flung the pebble afield, resentment flashing in his eyes momentarily.

"I did what my father had asked of me when I broke my promise to the girl I adored," he said, "I did it out of duty, out of obligation to the man who would one day make me King…"

Charles nodded his head, encouraging Harry to elaborate.

"But as each year had passed, the expression of betrayal on Katherine's face only burned brighter in my mind," Harry continued, "And no matter how many women I have seen gloriously naked before me, none have measured up to Katherine of Aragon standing by the fire on that dreadful day, wearing that hideous dress of wool."

Charles scratched at his stubbly cheek, contemplating how best to reply to the private confession of adoration and guilt.

But then Harry's voice took on a tone of disgust, hatred dripping from almost every word as he continued to admit his thoughts.

"Her mistreatment over the years has ached my heart, Charles, and as I grow older, I am becoming more aware of the many things that are wrong with my father's rulings –"

"—We should return, Harry," Charles stated quickly, interrupting his younger friend's flow of words and widening his eyes in warning, "Supper will be served soon."

Harry, understanding Charles' caution, looked over his shoulder to see three of the king's advisors leisurely entering the gardens as they mumbled quietly among themselves.

Thomas More, catching Harry's gaze on them, nodded in greeting, which Harry returned before turning back to Charles.

"Yes," Harry replied, "Let's return."

It had been a close call.

In his anger over Katherine's mistreatment, as well as his own, he had gotten carried away in his fury towards his father and his lap-dog, Dudley.

As they walked back towards the palace, he allowed his mind to wander to happier things to soothe his ire.

Since his return to court and her establishment as imperial ambassador, Harry and Katherine had interacted only a handful of times in as many months. Their conversations had been no more than passing pleasantries and remarks about the weather, but they would spark a floodgate of sensations within the young prince.

Seeing her walking towards him down a candle-lit hallway would raise the hairs on the back of his neck. The flicker of her pale eyelashes as she raised her eyes to meet his broke a sweat out on his palms.

He had bedded many ladies in the past few months, and not a single one had evoked such heart palpitations within him as Katherine of Aragon's ethereal look gave him.

And in more recent months Harry was more sure than ever before that no other woman would do for his wife.

Harry would often wonder of late if this was what it felt like to be in love, and he *had* hoped to ask Charles about it, who at twenty-three-years-old had been married twice already…

How he wished he could ask his mother about these feelings, for she and his father had been madly, passionately in love. Though their marriage had begun as nothing more than a political transaction – like most royal marriages – their mutual friendship and love had grown and fused together, just like the white and red roses of the Tudor crest, unifying the Yorks and Lancasters under one peaceful people.

He so wished to be a good heir to his father. He studied long and hard enough each day to hopefully achieve that.

But even if he may not be as learned or as kingly as Arthur would have been, Harry believed that as long as he had the woman he loved by his side, that he would rule well enough to make his mother and father proud.

There was nothing else for it, Harry decided as they entered the palace through a side entrance, all he could do was his utter best when the time comes.

And though he might fail at being the most perfect king as Arthur would have been, he believed that with Katherine of Aragon as his wife, he could at least aspire to be the perfect husband.

Katherine

I still think of him every day.
How could I not? He was a part of me.
Our souls will be united for eternity, no matter the distance between us now.
I still think of him every day.
And no matter what others might follow, he will always live on in my heart.

Chapter 5

February 1509

"I will not marry Eleanor," Prince Harry said as he stood tall before his father.

Negotiations had been underway for several months between Henry VII and the Holy Roman Emperor Maximilian for the seventeen-year-old Harry to become betrothed to nine-year-old Eleanor de Castille.

And Harry, unable to shake the feeling that he and Katherine of Aragon were destined for each other, could not allow his betrothal to another to go ahead.

His son had shot up in height in the past year, Henry Tudor noted wryly, though he was still a little shorter than his king, however much he tried to stretch himself.

"You will marry her," Henry replied coldly.

"I shall choose my own wife," Harry replied, puffing out his chest.

Henry Tudor had shortly recovered from his ailment the year before but had fallen ill again of late, and twice in the last few months he had been taken to lying in bed for several days, his rattly chest giving his physicians much cause for concern.

"While I live," Henry Tudor replied quietly, a warning, "You shall do as I command. And by God! You shall not marry that worthless Spanish *infanta*. You *will* marry Maximillians's granddaughter before I am laid to rest in my grave."

After the outburst, Henry spluttered a wet cough into his handkerchief, and Harry glared at him with narrowed eyes and a downturned mouth, his disgust and hatred for his father as clear as day.

He *had* come with the intention of containing his distaste for his father and his ruling, but the anger within the young man had succeeded in overriding his goal to be civil, and after years of repressed frustration and resentment towards him, he finally unleashed what he had been holding in for far too long.

"You'd best get on with it then," Harry hissed at his father and king, "*Die* already!"

April 1509

It would seem that it had been God's will all along that Prince Harry would marry Katherine of Aragon, for just two months after Harry's outburst, King Henry VII of England was dead.
Following the news of his father's death, Harry felt a strange weight lifting off his chest, followed by a sudden thrill as he realised that England's people would now look to him to rebuild the country.
A new order was on the rise. And with that came the need to signal to the people that his reign would be much different from his father's, and his first step would be to rid the court of those who had reached too high and caused too much discontent: it was finally time to seek vengeance on the man behind Harry's imprisonment.
And luckily for Harry, that same man had been at the very heart of Henry Tudor's extortions of the nobles over the years – the illegal coercion to pay bogus fines, the unlawful increase of bonds – they all gave the new king every right to issue the man's arrest.
The notorious, unpopular Edmund Dudley, the former President of the King's Council, was finished.

As requested in his will, the late king was lain to rest in Westminster Abbey to be reunited beside his most beloved wife, Elizabeth of York, both of them depicted in tomb effigies with their hands clasped together in prayer.

And with his death, his only surviving son, Harry the Prince of Wales, was declared King of England just shy of his eighteenth birthday with the full support and glee of his people.

And he would henceforth be known as King Henry VIII of England.

11th June 1509
Church of the Observant Friars, Greenwich Palace

Despite his father's direct command that Harry was *not* to marry the exotic princess of Spain, the new young king proclaimed far and wide that it had been the late Henry Tudor's dying wish that they be wed. And with his most trusted advisor, Edmund Dudley, imprisoned and soon to be executed there was no one to deny Harry's word.

For Harry – now to be styled Henry upon his father, and namesake's, death – would not begin his reign with negative attributions towards his chosen bride.

After years of torment and neglect at the hands of both their fathers, Katherine was finally heading towards her fate, a fate which would see her greatly rewarded for her perseverance.

With her constant and staunch belief that this would be her destiny, Katherine had managed to hold onto what her mother had always promised her: that the title of Queen of England would be hers.

With the Pope's blessing and papal dispensation already acquired years ago, the marriage ceremony went ahead without delay. And so, on a bright and sunny day, Katherine of Aragon walked down the aisle for the second time in eight years, her destiny so close within her reach.

Katherine was dressed in a white gown of silk stitched with gold thread, her long hair loose around her shoulders and down her back.

But as Henry stood at the altar watching Katherine make her way towards him, he thought her smile to be the most beautiful thing she was wearing.

Time stood still as she reached the altar, and her hand was gently placed over his. He peered at her standing beside him before the Archbishop of Canterbury, and when her eyes met his and a shy smile spread over her face, a bolt of lightning sparked within him. It was like he had been living in greyscale his entire life, and that she was the first thing he had ever seen in colour.

The ceremony was intimate, Katherine thought, compared to the one where she had married Arthur.

Her groom, this time, was more handsome however, for Arthur's allure had been his mind, and not his looks.

But Henry no doubt had other appealing qualities she would soon come to discover, and from this day forward she would have their whole lives together to uncover them.

She was aware that Henry harboured strong feelings towards her already, she had known ever since she had received the dozens of poems he had written her years ago; expressions of respect and promises of this very day.

Though, Katherine was yet to feel a true connection.

But as she stood hand-in-hand beside him, the sun beaming through the stained-glass windows of the church, Katherine believed that now their story would truly begin.

And there was no doubt in her mind, that it would be a story for the ages.

Later that day, after the young King Henry and his new bride had said their vows to one another, Katherine was being carefully prepared for the bedding ceremony.

"It will be different this time," Katherine considered quietly as her lady Catalina gently raised Katherine's chin and dabbed orange water down her neck.

"Yes, my lady," Catalina said, remembering Katherine's uneventful bedding ceremony with the late Prince Arthur, "You were both young that time. You were not expected to consummate right then and there."

"No," Katherine said pensively, hearing the words though Catalina hadn't spoken them: *But you will be expected to this time.*

She shivered then, and she covered herself with her arms as Catalina brushed her mistress' long wavy hair down her back. Katherine had not yet regained her former, fuller figure, the many years of impoverishment having left her slimmer than when she had first arrived in England nearly ten years ago.

She was grateful that her breasts continued firm, however, for she knew her young husband would appreciate that.

She only hoped he would look past her frail arms and flat belly, for nothing said infertility like a weak and bony woman. But Katherine knew that she would regain her fullness soon enough now that she was Queen and her days of praying for scraps of bread were permanently behind her. Her body would soon catch up with her new circumstances, and she would no doubt grant her young husband many, many children.

And yet, a knot of anxiety clenched her stomach, the prospect of being observed by dozens of people in her most vulnerable moment giving her pause.

"I am nervous," Katherine admitted in a whisper as she met her lady's eyes.

Catalina smiled and shrugged, as though it were the most common thing in the world – which, for a queen, it was.

"He is besotted with you, my lady," Catalina said with a teasing grin, "I am sure it will be over very quickly."

Katherine breathed a little laugh and then raised her arms for Catalina to pull her white satin and lace nightshift over her head.

Then they walked over to the marital bed, a great four-poster wood-carved bed beautifully decorated with rose petals.

Katherine climbed under the covers and lay on her back, her heart beating wildly as Catalina left to summon her new husband and the entourage that would witness their consummation.

The doors were swung open as though in slow motion, and as the many people entered, Katherine forced her gaze never to stray from Henry. And she was glad to see that he, too, only had eyes for her.

She communicated her nervousness to him with a small smile but his eyes were shinning with excitement and adoration, and Katherine's nerves ebbed slightly to think him so pleased with what he saw.

He disrobed eagerly, revealing a thin, white nightshirt that only just covered his buttocks and manhood. He pulled back the covers on his side and lay down beside her on his back, and Katherine was surprised to feel her heart skip a beat as his long, warm body pressed up against hers.

The two of them lay there, side by side, their hands folded together and resting over their chests as Archbishop William Warham blessed the marriage bed.

With the many onlookers surrounding the new couple, Catalina pulled down the veiled curtains on all sides of the bed, to offer them the illusion of privacy, at least.

Once the bishop fell silent, Henry turned his head to look at his wife, flashing his teeth in a boyish grin.

"Katherine," was all he said before reaching a hand up to caress her cheek.

They locked eyes as Henry rose up onto his elbow carefully, almost as if moving spontaneously would make her disappear, and Katherine's breath caught in her throat as his smile vanished and his expression changed into one of utter mesmerisation.

He loved her.

He truly loved her.

It was so clear to see.

He positioned himself gently on top of her, never once looking away from her face. Her eyes, her lips, her blushing cheeks.

His fixation with her was intoxicating, and Katherine's unease began to melt away underneath his gaze. It kept her mind from straying past the veiled curtains of their bed, and as he gently pressed his lips to hers, it was as though there were no witnesses after all; and it was suddenly just the two of them, husband and wife.

And then, ever so slowly, they were one.

Upon becoming king, Henry was pleasantly surprised to learn that England's treasury was not as sad and depleted as he had been made to believe due to his father's reputation of having been a miser. And he was gobsmacked to discover that, as the new king, he had just inherited a treasury bursting with gold.

It was a wonderful surprise, no doubt. But it only aided in irking the new king even more towards his late father, who had put Katherine through a world of misery due to King Ferdinand's refusal to pay the remainder of her dowry as though England had had some desperate need for it.

When, quite clearly, it hadn't…

So much could have been avoided if only his father had not been so tightfisted. So much heartache, so much lost time.

But now it was Henry's to use as he wished.

And he would make it up to his beautiful wife.

"I want us to be crowned together."

It was the day after their wedding, and Henry and Katherine were breakfasting together as newly married couples do.

"A joint coronation?" Katherine replied as she popped a sugared grape into her mouth.

Henry nodded enthusiastically, like the young man that he still was. Katherine couldn't help but smile at his excitement, and she reached her hand across the table and took a hold of his.

"If my lord husband wishes it."

"My lady grandmother," the new King Henry called in greeting later that day as Margaret Beaufort entered the council chambers.

Margaret smiled at her grandson and slowly made her way towards him, and Henry noticed that she was shuffling her feet.

His grandmother had always been thin, her piety calling for several days of fasting each week, but she had never looked quite so *frail* before.

Henry's mouth twitched with sorrow for his beloved grandmother, who he hoped would manage to overcome her grief.

It seemed Henry VII's death had hit his mother harder than it had hit his own son, and Henry wondered if he would soon get to love a son as much as Margaret Beaufort had so clearly loved hers.

Henry only hoped that *his* son would not grow to despise him quite as much as Henry had despised his own predecessor.

But that was an issue for a much later date.

"Please sit by the fire, grandmother," Henry said as he stood from his seat at the head of the table and offered it to Margaret.

The old lady *tsked*, "Do not ever give up your throne so easily, my boy," she said as she pulled out the chair to the king's right, "Much blood was spilled for your father to attain it."

She slowly lowered herself into the chair and sighed.

The room was empty save for the two of them and his new wife, Katherine of Aragon, who sat opposite Margaret and to the king's left, smiling at her pleasantly.

Margaret smiled back, her slack cheeks wrinkling considerably, "I am glad to see this day," she said warmly.

She watched as the young couple exchanged a shy look.

"Lady grandmother," the young king said then, before she could elaborate, too eager to voice his own thoughts than listen to an old lady's ramblings, "I have decided that my coronation should take place as a joint ceremony."

Margaret blinked quickly, "Joint?"

"A double coronation," Henry explained, "Katherine and I to be crowned Queen and King of England together."

He reached over and took his wife's hand then and squeezed it.

Margaret nodded, "It is a fine decision, Your Grace," she said, "but why have I been summoned?"

Henry smiled broadly at his grandmother, pleased with himself to have thought of it, for surely Margaret would be glad for this distraction. There were more important things to think of now than the old, dead king that had ruled before him.

"We wish for you to organize this grand occasion."

22nd June 1509

As was custom before a coronation, Katherine and Henry made their way to the Tower of London with a great procession, where they would stay before their joint crowning which was to take place in two days' time.

The streets of London were luxuriously decorated in anticipation of the coronation, houses and shops were adorned with intricate tapestries, some even with cloth of gold.

The crowds of people that had come to observe were so vast that railings had been put up along the streets to prevent the public from disturbing the parade.

Henry rode at the head of the procession on a horse adorned with gold damask and ermine, while above him a gold canopy was being carried by the Barons of the Cinque Ports. He wore

robes of crimson velvet trimmed with ermine over a gold jacket covered with diamonds, rubies, and emeralds.
Behind Henry, many lords, knights, and esquires followed on foot.
Katherine's procession followed Henry's.
Instead of a horse, Katherine sat in a litter which was supported by two white horses adorned with white cloth of gold.
She herself wore a gown of embroidered white satin, her wavy hair falling loose over her shoulders and down her back, similarly to her wedding day, though she wore a coronet with many rich stones on her head this time.
Catalina, as well as Katheirne's newly appointed ladies-in-waiting, Agnes Tilney and Lady Anne Hasting, followed their mistress in chariots.
Upon their arrival, they enjoyed a splendid banquet of many delicious dishes and fine music and dancing, which Henry and Katherine only observed from their seats at the high table, for they were exhausted from the enormity of the day.
The merriment was concluded in the late afternoon to allow time for prayer at St Stephen's Chapel, where the pious couple spent the next few hours in silence, before hurrying excitedly to their royal chamber to partake in a much less quiet activity.

24th June 1509
Westminster Abbey, London

It was finally here.
The day of their coronation was a Sunday and also Midsummer's Day.
The day in which Katherine would meet her destiny, the fate she had been promised all her life.
It was *just* in reach.
How wonderful it would be if she were with child *right now*.

A flutter of excitement burst in her chest then as she imagined hers and Henry's little baby in her belly, being crowned along with them in this magnificent display of unification.

Since their wedding night, the royal couple could not keep their hands off each other – though Katherine was yet to feel *love* for her new husband – and they would often steal quick moments alone together in between duties, unable to wait until the fall of night, and they'd arrive at their obligations breathing heavily from the exhilaration. And today had been no different, Katherine having slipped out of her chambers as soon as her ladies had finished dressing her to meet Henry behind the pillars in the far end of the darkened hallways.

With the adrenaline running through their veins, their couplings never did last long, both of them hanging on the edge of the precipice as soon as their lips met and ending in a mutual and muffled exclamation of pleasure just moments later, the secrecy of their daytime encounters only adding to their delight.

And later, as Henry and Katherine made their way to Westminster Abbey, their cheeks flushed and their eyes shining, the many onlookers put their glow down to excitement, none the wiser that it had derived from a morning of lovemaking.

The Barons of Cinque Ports held canopies over the royal couple as they walked along the path towards the abbey, the bright sunshine above illuminating their way.

Once inside the abbey, the noble king and his queen were met by the Archbishop of Canterbury and led down the aisle to their thrones.

The abbey was filled with clerics of the realm, members of the nobility and many lords and ladies, all beaming with delight to be witnessing such a momentous occasion. But none beamed quite as delightedly as the king's proud grandmother Margaret Beaufort as she observed their ascent from among the crowd.

She wiped a tear from her wrinkled face as the royal couple knelt before the archbishop, relieved to witness the Tudor dynasty's continuation.

Henry and Katherine were anointed according to sacred tradition and ancient custom by the archbishop, Henry being coronated with the crown of Edward the Confessor, while Katherine received the smaller crown of the Queen Consorts of England.

After many hours of ritual, the archbishop turned to the people.

"Do you take this most noble prince as your king and obey him?"

Without hesitation the crowd responded in unison and with devotion that they would.

When the ceremony was finished, they all returned to Westminster Hall, where a banquet had been arranged.

Their arrival was announced with a fanfare, the newly crowned King Henry VIII and Queen Katherine entering the hall hand-in-hand, and they made their way towards the high table to resume the celebrations, which would continue for many more days to follow.

Katherine

Destiny.
It is such a strange concept.
How can any of us truly know what God has in store for us.
Did he come to me in my dreams?
No.
Did he whisper to me while in prayer?
No.
To be the Queen of England – Was this the price I had to pay to achieve this destiny?
If that is the case, then I do not want it!
Take it back, oh Lord. Take it back!
Take it and restore to me what I have lost.
I would gladly exchange all the gold in the world for just one more day with him...

Chapter 6

29th June 1509

Just five days after Henry and Katherine had been crowned, the Lady Margaret Beaufort, Countess of Richmond and Derby, and the mother of the Tudor dynasty died at the age of sixty-six.

The news hit Henry hard, for his grandmother had always been his biggest supporter. And though he had been an orphan for many months already, it was only now that Henry felt truly without parental guidance.

"She will receive all the respect of a would-be queen," her grandson, King Henry VIII said, "In the Henry VII Chapel in Westminster Abbey."

Margaret's old friend and confessor Bishop Fisher nodded his balding head, "She was a great woman. Everyone that knew her loved her, and everything that she said or did became her."

A wave of fresh grief rushed through Henry then as the kind words were spoken.

For they could not have been more true.

August 1509

The twenty-four-year-old Queen Katherine stood before her looking glass in only her nightshift.

Her head was cocked to one side, her eyes focused on nothing and everything all at once as she ever so gently moved a hand up and down the length of her belly.

"Your dress, my lady," said Agnes Tilney, one of Katherine's new ladies.

She stopped short to see her queen in a pensive state before the mirror.

"Oh," Agnes said, as though she had interrupted her mistress in a most private moment.

Katherine turned to her lady and looked at the maroon dress she had carried in.

"I think I should like to wear something more vibrant today," the queen said with a pretty smile.

Upon her coronation, Katherine had adopted the pomegranate as her personal badge – a symbol of fertility since ancient times – and it would seem it was almost prophetic…

Agnes grinned and hurried to fetch the queen's most magnificent dress of royal purple silk without needing an explanation. For she, as well as the rest of her ladies, knew that their mistress had been waiting patiently for this day.

The day that she would break the news to her husband, that Katherine of Aragon was with child.

The last few months had been an up and down spiral of emotions for Henry.

Between the ascension into kingship, his marriage to the woman of his dreams – the *consummation!* – their joint crowning, the death of his beloved grandmother…

It had been a mixture of extreme joy and extreme heartbreak. But Henry should have known that he would not be wallowing in grief for long, for his wife was proving to be the most perfect specimen of a woman.

"With child?" the eighteen-year-old king said with a wide grin as he gently placed a hand on the small of Katherine's back, the other hand hovering protectively over her flat belly.

"I wanted to wait. To be sure," Katherine said with a grin as wide as Henry's own, "But yes, Henry. I am with child."

Her husband breathed a laugh then and tears welled in her eyes to see him so wholesomely happy, and then he took her face in between his big hands and planted a kiss on her lips.

People were watching – as they would do for the rest of their days – but Henry did not seem to care, and Katherine allowed herself to melt into him.

He continued to kiss her with such passion and yet so tenderly all at once, that for a moment, he made her feel like she was made of glass.

And it was in that very moment – as they stood surrounded by hundreds of courtiers, in a public setting that somehow felt like they were alone, that Katherine knew she was in love with her husband.

And, though her path to him had begun in tragedy, she thanked God that He had led her on this journey to find him.

To avoid the outbreak of plague in London, the king and queen left on progress.

Progress, Henry had learned during his hasty studies on how to *be* a king, was recognised as an important part of maintaining his authority as monarch. As England was mainly a rural kingdom with most people living and working on the land, to be seen by his subjects, the monarch was expected to venture out of London; and by visiting the localities, a monarch was presented to his subjects against a background of ceremony and ritualised splendour.

Henry had a clear vision of his kingship, and he wanted to model his rule on the great monarchies of France and Spain – a nation where the king was celebrated, as well as the latest ideas in arts and culture.

The royal progress travelled mainly by carriage, the journey being too far to travel completely by horse – though Henry would alternate between travelling on horseback in the mornings and continuing by carriage in the afternoons.

Katherine, however, since she was carrying the future of England in her womb, was required to travel by litter or by carriage with her ladies. But she didn't mind, for it was her duty as a wife and a queen to deliver her husband a healthy heir.

They stayed at Hamworth, Sunninghill, Woking, Farham, Esher, Enfield, and Waltham, and in each location, dozens of their people would gather simply to catch a glimpse of their new king and queen.

The royal couple would wave and sometimes give out coins.

The people would cheer, and women and children would come up to the queen's carriage and hold up plucked flowers to her, which she would take from the open window in exchange for a thankful smile.

Many would walk a mile with the royal progression, just to be able to later say that they had.

But before long, as the days turned colder, they began on their way back to London, and Katherine was secretly glad for it, for the many hours and days sitting and swaying within the queen's carriage was not aiding her nausea one little bit.

September 1509
Richmond Palace, London

The royal couple returned to London with their households, feeling glad to be back.

But none were more glad than the young king, who had a complaint to address with his physician.

"They feel heavy and there is aching."

Henry was standing before one of his physicians with his hose around his ankles and the physician kneeling before him.

"Pain?" the physician asked as he examined the king's testes.

Henry thought for a moment before replying. He didn't want to seem like a child complaining of mild aches and pains, but he was fearing for his ability to produce more heirs in the future.

"Not...really *pain*," Henry explained slowly, "But it is most uncomfortable."

The physician nodded and rose, waving his hands to indicate to the young king that he may dress himself.

Henry scooped his trousers up quickly, hoping he came across as nonchalant but knowing that his cheeks and neck were blushing fiercely.

"When does this...ache occur usually, Your Grace?" the white-haired physician asked casually.

Henry cleared his throat uncomfortably, "In the mornings it is especially...unpleasant. But I have noticed it occurs most often when –" he stopped and swallowed, feeling more awkward than ever, "when the queen is near me."

The old man smiled ever so faintly and nodded.

"My king," he said as he thought back on his own youth, so many years ago, "What you are experiencing is no ailment."

Henry exhaled loudly, relief that he was not dying washing over him.

"You are young. You are a man," the physician went on, "And men have certain needs women will never understand."

He made a note of something in his journal then before looking up at the king once more.

"Men have urges they need to fulfil to ensure their testes do not enlarge, as Your Grace's are doing."

"Enlarge?!" Henry said in horror.

The physician nodded sombrely, "While the queen is with child and unable to satisfy Your Grace's needs, I recommend that you take a mistress. To...relieve some of your aches."

"A mistress?" Katherine spluttered later that day when Henry had told her of the physician's counsel.

Henry took a step towards her, seized her hands in his, and looked into her eyes.

"I would never take a mistress," he reassured her, "You are the only lady for me. My queen. My *wife*. No other woman can compare, and I wish for no other than you."

Katherine smiled as her chest ached with love for this passionate man, and she raised their interlocked hands up and kissed his knuckles.

"You are the most noble king who ever lived," she told him, and she meant it.

Henry smiled coyly, still feeling bashful at his wife's praise.

"If my father taught me anything worth learning it was that a good king does not stray from his wife," Henry explained, "He never took a mistress. He and my mother loved each other fiercely."

His eyes glazed over with sadness as he thought of his deceased parents, sadness over his father's loss pinching Henry's heart for the first time since his death, "He may not have been the best father to me, but he showed me how to be a good husband. And I hope to be that to you."

"But your pain –" Katherine began, though she was elated to hear his confession of loyalty.

Henry dismissed her worry with a wave of his hand, "For you…I would endure endless suffering."

October 1509

The Perpetual Peace Treaty signed between England and Scotland seven years prior needed to be renewed due to the death of Henry VII.

But his successor Henry VIII was not as interested in peace as his father had been, and the young king – having been brought up with tales of military victory in France, and English overlordship of Scotland – was not especially eager to renew the treaty.

But, Scotland *was* the home of his older sister Margaret Tudor, who had been shipped abroad to marry the old King

James IV of Scotland to conclude this very Peace Treaty. And Henry thought that, for now at least, it would be wiser to maintain a friendly discord with his neighbouring country until he was well established and with at least one – or two – heirs in the nursery.

For though he was so far demonstrating himself as a composed and tranquil king, Henry had a hankering for war.

He had had it ever since he was a boy, when he had learned about Henry V's glorious successes in the Hundred Year's War against France, in his famous victory at the battle of Agincourt in 1415.

Henry *wanted* to be remembered for glorious battles and for claiming of new lands as Henry V had been.

Peace may have worked well for his father when he had been king, but even *he* had had his own fair share of fighting to attain the throne of England.

Henry *wished* for that same adrenaline rush that he imagined a young Henry Tudor had felt as he had defeated Richard III in the battle of Bosworth Field.

Henry knew he should concentrate the first few years of his reign on strengthening his position as King of England, to fix his feet firmly on the ground before a rash action would see him slip and fall.

But his youth was blinding his ability to think rationally, and if he couldn't engage in war with Scotland, France would have to do.

Because what Henry VIII desired above all else in this life as king, was conquest.

Though Henry VIII had inherited the throne of England with a general idea of what it meant to be king, he had not been prepared for the number of tedious meetings and discussions of foreign policies that were to take place.

When he ascended the throne, he had immediately been surrounded by experienced administrators who had served under his father: the Archbishop of Canterbury, William Warham, who had married Henry and Katherine some months ago, as well as the Bishop of Winchester, Richard Foxe, were among those brilliant men.

However, Henry – who was young and therefore looking to the future – had noticed that he did not always care for their counsel, especially not when they disagreed with his desire to engage in foreign warfare.

"It is an unnecessary expense," Richard Foxe told his king on one such tedious council meeting, "Not to mention a reckless one so early on in your reign, Your Grace, and without an heir to keep England safe."

The fresh-faced king sighed, "So there will be no war on France?" he asked, his red eyebrows raised in frustration, "No military glory, no new lands?"

"There is plenty of time for that, my king!" Warham answered, "More important than all that is a secure country. There are other ways we can begin to weaken France without engaging in war."

Henry sat up in his throne, suddenly intrigued.

"What other ways?"

Richard Foxe's secretary, a gentleman named Thomas Wolsey, observed from the corner of the room as the young king leaned forward eagerly at the prospect of aggravating France, and the man narrowed his eyes in thought.

He had previously been appointed a chaplain during Henry VII's reign and had since been slowly climbing the social ladder through his connections and his brilliant mind, but mostly through his ability to observe.

"Pit Spain and France against one another," Warham said in response to his king, "Let them bicker and squabble at each other while England sits back and amounts her strength. And then, when we are secured and they are walking on shaky ground, then would be the time to strike."

Henry's eyes went wide with excitement at the prospect of battle, "How long before we can make plans of invasion?"
Warham and Foxe exchanged a look and suddenly laughed, the way only older men laughed at younger, more foolish, men – a deep guffaw of superiority and pitying arrogance.
Foxe's secretary, Wolsey, witnessed from the far corner how the young king's jaw ticked at the men's laughter, and he could almost feel Henry's humiliation coming off him like the heat from an open flame.

"It would be years yet, Your Grace," Foxe replied after he caught his breath.

"Yes, my king," Warham agreed, "Years. Years yet."
Henry sat back slowly as he nodded, his jaw still set tight at the men's mockery of him.

"Right you are," Henry said, his tone clipped. Then he rose, "Well, then. I shall return to more important matters, gentlemen. You may retire to your dark and musty chambers and try to come up with ways to cause discord between France and the Hapsburg Empire."
The two old men stood and nodded their white heads, "Your Grace," they mumbled, before walking out the door, Thomas Wolsey following behind.
Henry watched them leave, his eyes fixed on the men's backs as they left.
And then Thomas Wolsey looked back over his shoulder and met the king's hard stare. He offered the king a warm smile and a bow of his head, making sure to maintain eye contact and to offer the king a moment of encouragement following that instance of great humiliation.

Following Wolsey's indication of support for his king, Henry had shown Wolsey his favour by sending him the first cuts of the finest meat dishes during banquets and ushering him over to sit beside the king to partake in drinking and private conversation.

Henry had taken to the man quickly, seeing him as a source of quiet wisdom without the overbearing arrogance the Archbishop Warham and Bishop Foxe had. And before long, Henry had appointed Thomas Wolsey as the Royal Almoner – a post that put him in charge of the crown's charitable giving – and which automatically granted him a position on the King's Council.

Thomas Wolsey's influence at court continued on the rise, and with his newly acquired friendship with the king, there was no knowing how high he might dare to reach.

November 1509

Ever since Katherine of Aragon had first felt the earth-shatteringly joyous movement of her baby as it swirled around in her belly, she had been suddenly plagued by the shrill and devastating sound of a crying infant.

It had begun in the deepest chasms of her dreams some weeks ago, fading almost immediately into the darkest folds of her subconscious as soon as she awoke.

But as the days went on, the cries became a permanent fixture in her mind as soon as she closed her eyes at night.

She couldn't bring herself to tell her lord husband for fear that he would worry for their child.

But she knew their child was strong. Katherine could feel him moving inside the dome of her belly each day, kicking joyfully and dancing whenever she sang.

Their child was happy.

It was not screaming in anguish inside her womb.

No.

This screaming… it had to be another child.

But no matter how hard she tried, Katherine could never find the source of the screaming in her dreams.

"How do you feel, my lady?" her husband asked her cheerfully one morning as they walked together towards the jousting tiltyard in the far field behind the palace, which Henry had ordered to be custom built just weeks after their joint coronation.

"I am well, Henry," she replied, though she had hardly slept a wink last night, and she was sure that he could tell by the purple bags under her eyes.

As if he'd heard her thoughts, Henry reached a slender finger up then and poked her just above her cheek, frowning as he did so, "You do not look well."

Katherine flinched slightly.

This man had seen her naked.

This man had made love to her, slept beside her, made a child with her, urinated in the piss pot as she watched – horrified – from across the room.

But that prodding of her tired face. It had felt like a violation, like an insult.

And for the first time – perhaps due to the lack of sleep – Katherine felt pestered by her younger husband.

But she clenched her teeth together and said nothing, as a good wife ought to.

The king and queen took their seats underneath the canopy, the Princess Mary sitting beside her sister-in-law, as the courtiers continued standing, surrounding the jousting tiltyard at a respectable distance, and overlooking the two large octagonal brick towers.

It was a dry day for November – which was what had led the king to demand for outdoor activities – but suddenly Katherine wished for nothing more than for it to rain, so that she might excuse herself from the public eye and her husband's scrutiny for just one moment.

The tournament began with cheering and applause, one knight after another getting knocked off their horse, but always recovering quickly, as young men did.

After a while Henry rose from his cushioned seat beneath the canopy and excused himself from the entertainment, claiming urgent matters in need of attending.

Katherine, who knew of her husband's plan, smiled faintly at her sister-in-law Mary beside her as the young princess watched her brother hurry away.

The yet heirless king had been urged continuously by his Privy Council not to partake in dangerous activities, such as jousting.

But Henry, having been forbidden to do as he pleased for far too long under his father's reign, believed it was high time to indulge in his favourite past time, after so many years of the absence of fun.

But it was not only about enjoyment. Jousting allowed for those who partook to display their aptitude for chivalric arts; to show off their gallantry, vigour, and strength in this masculine sport.

And Henry was all about showing off his prowess to his queen and his court.

As if out of nowhere, an unknown knight suddenly appeared from out of one of the many tents dotted around the tiltyard. He was taller than most men, and he was covered from head to toe in armour, his visor already down to conceal his identity.

With a wave of his hand as he approached the horses, the knight announced his intent to partake, and he swung himself effortlessly onto a large, black horse, as though his armour weighed practically nothing.

For the following half an hour, the mysterious knight continued undefeated, showing great skill as he unseated rider after rider, amassing the most points by expertly striking the tip of his lance directly against the opponent's boss each time.

The crowd was in awe, ladies clapped as they smiled open-mouthed, in admiration for this mysterious rider, and

Katherine breathed a laugh and shook her head at their naivety.

The strange knight – Henry – dismounted then, swinging his long legs off his steed.

The crowd held their breath as he raised his hands to remove his helmet, and once he whipped his unmasked head back and shook his red locks from his face, the dozens of courtiers called with amazement that this extraordinary jouster, this formidable rider, was their young king himself.

The athletic king was a sight to behold. One Katherine would surely never tire of.

Standing tall at six-foot-two, Henry towered above most men of the court. His limbs were long and wiry and in recent months, Katherine had noticed him becoming more and more muscular.

She could hear many ladies in the crowd gushing over him as they clapped.

An 'Adonis' they were calling him, and Katherine thought how lucky she was. Not only had she obtained her destiny as Queen of England, but her political marriage had blossomed into a love match. And now she was carrying the product of their love within her – the very future of England.

Katherine inhaled deeply and placed a protective hand over the small curve of her belly just as Henry found her gaze through the hundreds of cheering people and gifted her a wink.

Just then, as Henry began walking over to his opponent who sat defeated on the dirty ground, and the people around her continued cheering, all sound suddenly caved in on Katherine.

It was as though her ears had suddenly lost all ability, and her surroundings took on an eery, slowed motion.

She could see the courtier's hands clapping together oh so slowly, their faces pulled into many expressions of joy but somehow frozen almost to a standstill.

And it was then that the echoed crying began. Far in the distant shadows of her mind.

She could hear the same screaming that had been torturing her in her dreams, the screams of a lost little infant somewhere in the void.

The sound was coming from all angles, and Katherine whipped her head from side to side, hoping to identify the source of the wails.

She had to find this baby, this sad, desperate child which was no doubt scared and lonely, perhaps even hungry and cold.

Katherine rose from her seat in one swift motion.

And suddenly, as though she had emerged from under water, the screaming was gone and the many people surrounding her returned to their normal motions, their calls of praise for the king encircling her once again.

"I do not feel well," the queen told her most trusted lady, Catalina, then as she turned to her, "Take me to my cham –"

But before she could utter the words, Katherine fell into her lady's arms, unconscious.

Katherine

I sit up with a jolt, startled awake from what must have been another dream of him.
I can still feel the weight of his body on my chest.
I remember now that the first time he had lain on me he had weighed less than I'd imagined he would.
But he had been strong...
He had been many things and would've been many more – King of England among them.
Despite not having known him for long I did know that one thing: that he had been strong.
He just hadn't been strong enough to survive.

Chapter 7

"Her Grace is well, your highness," the king's physician informed the worried young husband as he paced up and down outside the queen's chambers, "She is fatigued. The babe is no doubt draining Her Grace's energy, as is natural. She is now resting."

"Should I go in –?"

The physician held up his hand, "I would not recommend it, my lord. The queen *needs* sleep."

Henry frowned with worry for his beloved wife and child, but he nodded his head, grateful for the older man's wisdom.

The king hung his head and the two men walked away from the queen's chambers side by side in silence, the physician's robes swishing gently, the sound comforting the young king.

"I shall arrange for a magnificent masquerade," Henry said all of a sudden then, his head snapping up, his blue eyes shining with excitement for the idea, "Yes! That should aid in lifting the queen's spirits! I shall display my love for her through the great tradition of disguising."

He turned his face to the wrinkled physician and grinned, "Would that not be splendid?"

"The physicians have instructed Your Grace to rest," Katherine's lady-in-waiting, Anne Hastings, said as she brought a silver tray to the queen's bed.

Anne, Lady Hastings, had recently joined the court upon Katherine's coronation to serve among the queen's household. At two years older than Katherine and recently married to her second husband, Anne and the queen had quickly bonded over their shared similarities.

As the daughter of Henry Stafford and Catherine Woodville, the Lady Anne was a noble lady of royal blood through her relation to the former Queen of England, Elizabeth

Woodville, and had been a great match for her new husband George Hastings.

Now, as the lady placed the tray on the bedside table, Katherine sat up and leaned back against the pillows, a faint smile of thanks on her lips.

"We are under strict orders from the king to keep you abed," Anne Hastings told her mistress as she carefully arranged the silver tray to be within Katherine's reach.

The queen exhaled deeply, "I must remain abed?" she asked, her eyes glancing down at the plate of food and cup of small ale.

Anne nodded, her small mouth pulled down at the sides in compassion for her queen, "But look!" she said, pointing to a red rose on the tray, hoping to lift the queen's spirits.

Katherine smiled faintly, "From the king?" she asked as she leaned over and picked it up carefully before frowning down at its stem, "It has been de-thorned."

Anne sighed dreamily, "A true knight, our king," she breathed before turning away to attend to her other chores.

Katherine brought the flower to her nose and inhaled, "Yes," she mumbled to herself, "A true knight."

Though Henry would never admit to it, he had inherited his paranoia from his father.

It wasn't a terribly negative attribute to have, he told himself, especially not for a young king whose hereditary claim to the throne of England was weak to begin with – the Tudor line being only fairly new compared to most noble bloodlines.

His father's claim to the English throne had always been weak, Henry Tudor having grown up as an exile for most of his life as the last Lancastrian heir during the thirty-year-long War of the Roses, the Cousin's War.

He had claimed the throne through battle, not through legacy. And certainly not for his pedigree.

Becoming King of England with such a knowledge, that he had been somehow *less than,* brought with it the paranoia that Henry had grown up observing in his father.

And he was finally beginning to understand just *why* Henry VII had always been so…distrusting.

While Henry had married a strong princess and formed a formidable alliance with one of the strongest nations in the world, England would never be fully safe from invasion.

And though he had managed to put a child and heir into his legal wife exceptionally soon after their wedding, he would not be fully safe as King until he had – at *least* – two male heirs thriving in the nursery.

"England is surrounded by enemies on all sides, Scotland to the north and France to the south," the young king said enthusiastically to his council, "Yes, we have signed the Peace Treaty with Scotland that forbids either of us from invading the other –"

"Under pain of excommunication from the Pope himself, your highness," one of the older men interrupted brazenly.

Henry nodded, "But it is not enough. And I have decided to expand our naval capacity." he concluded.

Henry VIII may be young, but he had learned from his father to always keep a watchful eye on all possible outcomes.

He may not have always agreed with his lord father while he had been alive. He may not even have liked him.

But the man *had* known how to keep the crown despite his flimsy claim.

And by God! Henry would not allow his personal dislike of his late father cloud his judgement into acknowledging the truth: that Henry VII had been a smart ruler.

The design of two new warships was approved and preparations were made for them to be built in Portsmouth in due course.

The designing of the two ships had brought Henry great joy, and their development, as well as the approaching arrival of his heir, meant the young king was on a constant high.

It had been decided that one of the ships would be larger than the other, and while both were to be carracks designed for war, the smaller one would not be built to carry guns.

But the other – and this was already Henry's favourite, though it wasn't even built yet – would carry up to eight large guns.

"It will require a new design feature –" Henry had been told in confused protest, "It has not been done before."

But the king had insisted, "Do it."

The king's state-of-the-art design was later approved, the new feature being named 'gun ports.'

The Tudor Rose and the Pomegranate were to be displayed on the ship's badges, to celebrate the royal couple and to signify the power of the Tudor dynasty.

All was going to plan.

And Henry could hardly contain his excitement.

18th January 1510
Westminster Palace, London

As his wife had continued to lay abed for the remainder of the month of December, emerging only to attend the Christmas festivities, Henry had taken it upon himself to organise a surprise masquerade for his queen.

His aim had been to cheer her from this gloomy time of early confinement, to show her that while they were parted, he was always thinking of her.

Disguised as Robin Hood, the king and twelve of his closest companions, including one Charles Brandon, burst into the queen's chambers one morning, boldly and unannounced.

Henry had, of course, made sure to pick a time when he knew she would be decent but had failed to account for her morning prayer, and upon their entrance, a collective gasp escaped the group of ladies who, Henry noticed too late, had been engrossed in silent worship.

Henry stopped in his tracks to find his wife kneeling in prayer at her prie-deux, her hands clasped together tightly, her rosary beads hanging from her fingers.

Should he withdraw and apologise for his disruption of her private moment with God?

No, surely the whole point was to catch her off guard. He could not simply turn around now and come back later.

It was now or never.

God would forgive him. After all, he was the king!

"What is the meaning of this?" the Lady Anne Hastings called suddenly as she rose to her feet from behind her kneeling queen, one hand pressed against her chest in shock.

Underneath Henry's hood and mask, he was grinning. He had no doubt that his entourage's attire of black cloaks, bows, arrows, and swords incited some confusion in the women, perhaps even a flash of fear, even if only for a moment.

And Henry realised then that he liked it.

"Fear not, my fair maidens," the king called, his voice slightly deeper in an effort to disguise himself further, "No harm shall come to you!"

And with that Henry turned on his twelve companions and played out a well-choreographed sword fight.

The queen's ladies squealed with delight as they rose and took some steps back to sit by the windows, allowing their sham trespassers more space for their performance.

Catalina helped the expecting Katherine up from her prie-deux and fussed over her as she led her to a cushioned seat by the fire.

The queen and her ladies watched the masquerade intently, gasping and clapping whenever was appropriate, their faces bright with smiles and giggles throughout.

Katherine mirrored her lady's reactions perfectly, encouraging her dear husband as she knew she should, for it was a great display of adoration and courtship indeed.

But despite her demonstration of joy, Katherine was utterly desperate for the unexpected entertainment to come to an end so that she may return to her prayer.

Because Henry had indeed interrupted her moment with God – a moment where she had been asking Him to give her a sign that her child was safe.

For she hadn't felt him moving in the safety of her womb now for three whole days.

31st January 1510

The queen's screams were a mixture of agony and despair as she laboured her baby into the world, and though this was but her first pregnancy, Katherine knew that her labour had come too soon.

She knew it from her ladies' stunned faces as her waters had suddenly broken in the middle of her morning prayer.

She knew it from the heavy silence that befell the birthing chamber as she pushed.

But above all else, she knew it from the dreadful feeling of emptiness that had taken hold of her heart.

"Lay back now, your highness, and breathe," one of the plump midwives said before beginning to demonstrate how she wished for Katherine to breathe, the midwife's mouth shaped into a round 'o' as she exhaled rhythmically.

Katherine watched the midwife and copied her exactly.

But she knew that it was pointless.

For none of *this* – the midwives, the pallet bed, the birthing ropes, the *breathing* – none of it would save her baby's life… He was already dead.

After what felt like an eternity – the queen's energy failing quickly from the ordeal – with one great, final push, her baby was born.

Katherine half exhaled, half screamed as she fell back against the pillows, her eyes squeezed shut.

She didn't want to see.

She couldn't.

To see him, her baby, born sleeping, born *dead* – it would be too painful to bear.

The hot tears seeped from the corners of Katherine's closed eyes then, the raw emotion being too vast to contain, and then her mouth twisted downwards into an ugly grimace, and she wailed.

She wailed to block out the deafening silence of the room, to fill in the blank moments that should have sounded brightly with the cries of a newborn baby's squeals.

Then Katherine rolled onto her side and made herself as small as she could, folded into a foetal position, her body shaking with unbearable grief, devastation, and sorrow.

But worse than everything else was the overwhelming feeling of failure.

"Your Grace," a soft voice whispered near her, and Katherine's eyes fluttered open, her vision blurred with misery.

Standing before her was one of the midwives.

And she was holding a tiny, tiny, *tiny,* bundle wrapped in blankets.

"Does Your Grace wish to hold her?"

The queen had been cleaned and made comfortable before being put to rest in the comforts of her royal bed.

She lay on her side, her belly still swollen before her as she gazed almost unblinkingly into her newborn baby's little face.

It was all she could see of her. Her tiny body being wrapped tightly in a blanket, as though it even mattered that she be kept warm.

It didn't…

It didn't matter at all.

But Katherine was grateful nonetheless for whoever had tenderly swaddled her sleeping infant, for this way at least, Katherine could pretend – for even just one moment – that her baby had survived.

With her head resting on the pillow, Katherine continued simply to stare at her baby's perfect little face.

The ghostly white eyelashes lining the crease of her closed eyes.

The button nose, the cheeks.

The pouty, perfect little lips.

But of course, there were other things to see too.

The translucent skin, the tiny blue veins beneath it.

The purple hue…

All the signs that her child was, in fact, not living were right there, staring her in the face.

And yet she could not bear to be parted from her.

Katherine lifted her hand slowly then. She just wanted to touch her, to feel her skin against her own, in the hope that she could take one memory of her firstborn child with her for eternity.

She brushed a finger along the curve of her baby's cold cheek…

And it was enough. Enough to break her, enough to crush her soul and grind her spirit into dust.

Surely this was the worst pain one could possibly undergo.

This – right here – this moment when you become a mother, and in that same breath…don't.

Katherine

Happiness.
It has been ripped from me like the peeling skin off a finger. And yet I keep picking at the raw, open wound every time I revisit that day. That day when I lost everything...
But now it is time.
Time to store it away in a box and close the lid, for I do not think I will survive if I keep holding on.
Too many years have gone by in mourning. Too many years lost in the haze of grief. The death of a child will do that to you...
And so I close the lid on my past, and as I do – as cut open as I am – I can feel myself shaping into something new.

Chapter 8

"The queen is recovering well," the old physician informed King Henry and the newly appointed Royal Almoner, Thomas Wolsey, a week later, "But there is something that gives me pause."

Eighteen-year-old Henry VIII raised his head from his hands in one sharp motion, fear for his wife's wellbeing encircling his every thought.

His eyes were red-rimmed from many hours of crying, his complexion ashen, his under-eyes dark; and the doctor's jaw twitched to see the young man so visibly distraught.

This was not the way a king ought to present themselves to his subjects. But, of course, it was not his place to criticise his monarch.

In fact, it was *no one's* place to criticise him.

The physician flicked his gaze to Wolsey who stood beside Henry, a look passing between the two older men briefly.

He was everywhere of late. Anywhere the king went, Thomas Wolsey was there beside him to offer him sound advice. Though, at the age of thirty-six years old, Thomas Wolsey was no more wise than the next man, and yet for some reason it was as if the king had adopted him as some kind of father figure.

The old physician opened his mouth to speak, but Thomas Wolsey swiftly turned towards his king then and planted both hands on the monarch's shoulders.

"My king, you must pull yourself together. And swiftly too!" Thomas Wolsey said sharply, to which the physician's eyes widened in horror.

He had heard of the man's rash way of speaking to the young king but had never before experienced it in person.

It was most unspeakable to behold.

But then Henry sniffed and stood from his seat with a straight back and a less defeated gaze.

Wolsey certainly had a way with the king.

"You are the sovereign lord, our leader!" Thomas Wolsey continued, "You are the backbone of this country. You must show strength in times such as these, and not give into your earthly desperation."

The young king nodded at Wolsey, sniffed once more, loudly, and swallowed his despair and his phlegm.

"Speak," Henry said then, looking over Wolsey's shoulder and directly at the physician, his voice firm.

The physician licked his lips and blinked slowly, the disturbing occurrence before him having briefly fogged his mind.

"The queen," the old physician said, "her belly is not deflating as is expected, my lord. I believe good news is in order."

"Twins?!" Katherine said as she looked down at her still-swollen belly.

"Isn't it wonderful?" her husband said, his face beaming at her in that boyish way of his, as though the potential of another baby erased the loss of the other.

But Katherine nodded and forced a smile, for of course it was joyful news indeed.

She looked down at her belly once again, unconvinced, and ran a hand over it, "I pray God it is a boy," she said.

When what she really meant was, *I pray God it lives.*

February 1510

King Henry was overjoyed at the news that the sorrow which had followed the death of their daughter would not be allowed to consume them. For God had sent them a gift of hope.

The physician's news that Katherine continued with child despite their tragic loss was proof enough for Henry to believe that God was watching over them, and that no matter what was thrown their way, that he and Katherine would endeavour through it together.

And so, when the queen's belly remained swollen and the physicians continued pleasantly surprised by her development, Henry ordered for furniture to be built for the baby's nursery.

A cot, a rocking horse, tiny wooden chairs, all was to be newly built for his heir.

For nothing would be too good for this miracle child.

5th March 1510

The queen re-entered into confinement to await the birth of her *other* baby.

The one she hadn't known about.

The one she hadn't felt moving inside her.

The one she had no connection to whatsoever.

The one she knew did not exist.

But the physicians kept insisting that he was real, and that he was growing, healthy and strong.

And they kept on insisting and insisting.

Even as Katherine told them that they were wrong.

And even as Katherine's monthly bleeds returned.

17th March 1510

The queen's belly finally began to deflate in the weeks that she and her ladies continued in confinement, and it was then that the physicians would begin to agree that they had, in fact, been wrong.

Henry, upon hearing the news that there was no other baby after all, immediately rushed to his wife despite the fact that men were not permitted into the dark and stuffy birthing chambers during the queen's confinement.

"Let me to her. Let me to my wife!"

Katherine heard her husband's anxious commands before the door was swung open to reveal a grief-stricken Henry, his eyes roaming the chambers, shining with devastation, until he found his queen standing by the window.

As Henry made his way towards her, the queen's ladies looked from one to another, silently questioning what they ought to do. Were they to be dismissed from the birthing chambers before the priest had given his blessing for them to? But their uncertainty was answered when the king, without tearing his eyes from his queen, ordered them all to leave.

"Out!" he called over his shoulder, "All of you!"

The ladies barely curtsied before scuttling out the door and Henry did not even wait for the door to be closed behind them before crushing his lips over Katherine's desperately, as though he had been awaiting this moment for months.

Which, in fact, he had.

"I am so sorry," Henry mumbled against Katherine's mouth in between kisses, his brow furrowed with grief, "I am so so sorry."

He swivelled her round gently then to untie her dress at the back, and he pressed warm kisses along her neck as his hands fumbled with the knots.

Unable to fully untie them, Henry groaned in frustration and spun her back around to face him, pulling her corset down forcefully instead, the loosened cords allowing for it to budge enough that Katherine could shimmy the rest of it down over her slightly rounded belly and hips.

"You shouldn't be here," Katherine whispered hoarsely as his eyes roamed over her body, "It is forbidden."

Henry raised his gaze and locked eyes with her, "Do you want me to leave?"

Katherine stared back as she stood before him, naked and vulnerable, her belly still sporting a little roundness, the only proof that was left that they had had a baby at all.

Despite the swell, she believed the rest of her body to be healed from the ordeal.

And yet, her soul continued broken.

But in that moment, Katherine believed that they both needed this – each other – to begin their journey towards recovery, and though she was not yet out of confinement, who better than to break this rule with than the king himself.

"No," she replied, "I don't want you to leave," her voice so small she wondered for a moment if he had even heard her.

But before she could second guess herself, Henry scooped her into his strong arms and led her blindly towards the bed.

Though Henry had been desperate for the physical release for many months, he had tried to be as gentle and as careful as on their very first night together, and Katherine had never felt more in love with her husband than in that moment. But despite his best efforts, his kisses grew frantic and his hands traversed her body in a way that seemed to want to tear her apart even as they held her together.

Their love making had hurt Katherine a little after all, but she had willingly endured the ache until the end, their mutual need to repair their souls outweighing her need for comfort.

April 1510

The following week, Katherine had finally been officially released from her confinement, her belly having completely deflated and the physicians apologising profusely for their error in judgement.

"There will be others," Henry soothed his queen one evening as they lay in each other's arms in the queen's bed.

There had been no intimacy since their reconnection the week before, but that did not stop the royal couple from comforting each other, cuddling up beneath the sheets as the fire crackled soothingly in the fireplace.

Henry stroked Katherine's hair in slow, repetitive motions as her head lay against his muscular shoulder, both of them staring up at the wood panelled ceiling, decorated beautifully with careful carvings of the Tudor rose in each panel.

"I know…" Katherine replied, barely above a whisper.

Henry moved slightly then so that he could look at her, "You know I love you, don't you?" he said as his pale blue eyes searched her face.

Katherine stared up at him, this young king, so full of life, full of promise, full of hope.

She nodded.

"Then worry not," he said with a strained smile, concluding the matter as settled, "We shall have more babies. Dozens of them. I can see them in our future, dearest Katherine."

He was hurting too, Katherine reminded herself then. His body had not gone through the suffering, but her husband, too, had lost a child that he had loved.

And she needed to comfort him as he was comforting her.

They needed to hold onto *each other* now, two rafts in this stormy sea called life.

He bent his head down and kissed her, a quick peck on the lips, then they simply stared into each other's eyes, saying far more with that look than they could have ever communicated through words: that they both continued heartbroken over their loss, that they missed their daughter as though she had taken a piece of their hearts with her.

And with that look, Katherine knew she could begin to heal, knowing that Henry too, was utterly broken inside.

He kissed her again then, not a quick peck this time, but a gentle and slow caress of her lips with his. He did it again and

again, his arms wrapping around her when she began to cry silently.
They held each other for hours, kissing and cuddling until the fire had died down and the darkness had swallowed them up. There had been no intimacy.
And yet, it had been the most intimate moment Katherine had ever experienced.

"Without the security of an heir, it would be wise to renew our peace treaty with France," Thomas Wolsey said to the king one evening as the two of them wandered the palace, deep in thought.
Henry groaned at Wolsey's advice, for Henry had been eager to go to war.
But he nodded, "I shall get a renewed document drawn up for me to sign as the new King of England."
Wolsey bowed his head in agreement, "It is the safest option during these times while your highness adjusts to kingship."
At the remark, Henry shot him a look through narrowed eyes. He enjoyed Wolsey's company greatly, and Henry sought knowledge from the more worldly man, but he would not stand to be insulted, no matter how miniscule the insult may be. Or how accurate.
Wolsey noticed the young king's change in mood and quickly scrambled to reaffirm his position as growing favourite, "If Your Grace would permit it, I would be honoured to offer my services to the reworking of the treaty, to cast an eye over the finished product before your highness were to sign?"
Henry shrugged, suddenly disinterested in the topic of conversation as he noticed his friend, Charles Brandon.

"Charles!" Henry called, a great grin brightening his face.
Charles and his companion William Compton, who too was a good friend of the king's, approached.

"How would you like to go hunting?" Henry asked them, breaking free of Wolsey's company, "I am all talked out. And if I am to be denied my war in France, I need to quench my thirst for bloodshed some other way."

Peace with France was renewed as England's peace with Scotland had been just a few months prior, and it meant that Henry's reign and country would be safe from all sides for another year.

Following this, despite his slight affront a few days prior, Thomas Wolsey continued in the king's good graces, being present whenever possible to offer the young monarch his opinion.

Henry appreciated Wolsey's forthcomingness, his ability to speak plainly and openly to the king without appearing condescending or superior.

Henry VIII appreciated the man's knowledge greatly, especially when it meant Henry did not need to do much of his own thinking because of it.

To show his favour the king continued to bestow gifts and titles onto Wolsey, having most recently granted him the title of Registrar to the Order of the Garter, among others. With his continuous increase of responsibilities, Wolsey was slowly but surely relieving the king from some of his kingly duties, something which Henry appreciated considerably, for it allowed him more time to pursue other activities. Activities which involved much more entertainment than sitting in a dark room counting coins or signing papers.

"I have no mind for dull discussions of taxes and the poor harvest," Henry had told Charles Brandon one day after announcing to his council that he would no longer be made to sit – day in, day out – in the dark, stuffy council chamber only to discuss mundane things, "Talk does not get the blood pumping as action does."

Instead, the king would use his time more wisely, spending the bright Spring days on horseback or hawking in the field before the palace.

Since the king's incognito participation in the jousting tournament some months prior – where he had succeeded in showing off his unmatched skill – Henry had been able to convince his fearful advisors that he would be safe to partake in outdoor pursuits once more, whether he had an heir in the nursery or not.

Henry enjoyed nothing more than to take to the outdoors with his comrades Charles Brandon and William Compton, returning hours later breathing heavily and grinning contentedly – the day well spent!

And upon his return, after having quenched his thirst for hunting, hawking, and jousting, Henry wished only for the embrace of his lady, after a long day of being parted.

And after some time, their new routine had succeeded in healing their sorrow – time and distraction being the physicians most trusted treatment for heartache – and the royal couple overcame their mourning for their lost daughter. And in their healing, a few months after their loss, they found themselves desperately ready for a brighter chapter in their lives.

Chapter 9

May 1510

Katherine could not stop being sick.

And along with the nausea came the return of the haunting wails of a baby.

The rosebushes in the gardens outside her window were in full bloom, and the smell of them were not agreeing with her of late.

"It smells like they are rotten," Katherine mumbled to her lady Catalina in between retches, the faint cries of an infant echoing in her subconscious.

Her lady-in-waiting Agnes walked over to the open window and craned her neck, leaning over the sill, "They are most certainly not rotten. They look lovely."

Catalina rolled her eyes at her queen and Katherine sighed, "Close the window, please, Agnes."

Agnes did as she was told and cringed at the sound of Katherine vomiting yet again.

"Shall I fetch you some broth, Your Grace?" her other lady, the Lady Anne Hastings said as she approached Katherine.

The queen nodded as Catalina wiped the spit from Katherine's chin, and Anne picked up her skirts obediently and hurried out the door.

"I must have eaten something foul," the queen mumbled groggily as she watched Anne leave from the corner of her eye and Agnes taking herself off to the other room.

Catalina raised one eyebrow knowingly while she rubbed her mistress' back gently, "Or –"

"Don't say it!" Katherine interrupted suddenly, though the crying in her mind had already confirmed what she did not want to admit, "Don't speak the words. If I am it is still early, and I do not wish to even consider it."

Her lady pressed her lips together in thought, her silence spurring Katherine to elaborate.

"I am not ready to be with child again," she whispered, admitting her apprehension.

Catalina nodded, understanding her queen's fear.

"We shall tell the court you ate something foul," her lady said, offering Katherine a companiable smile.

The queen nodded and smiled back briefly before another wave of nausea hit and she returned to spewing into the bowl, grateful to have a true friend in her lady.

June 1510

With Katherine's nausea continuing strong in the following weeks, it was quickly becoming impossible to maintain the tale that she had simply eaten something foul, and rumours that the queen was with child once again began to spread throughout the court.

"Is it true?" Henry asked her excitedly one morning over breakfast, having heard the court gossip, "Are you with child?"

Katherine inhaled deeply as she put down her cup of small ale and looked around at the servants that stood in all corners like statues, "I did not wish for you to find out through gossip..."

Henry waved away her comment, "So the talk is true!?" he asked rowdily, but he was grinning from ear to ear, flashing a row of white teeth.

Katherine returned his smile and nodded, "I believe I am, yes. Though it is early still."

Henry was up from his seat in one fluid motion, holding out his hands to her. Then he helped her rise as gently as though she were a fragile flower and pulled her to him.

"This time will be different, dearest Katherine," he mumbled protectively as he held her, "I will pray God each day to keep you and the baby safe. I will promise Him

anything in return for a healthy child, boy or girl, it does not matter," he pulled away then and looked at her, grinning, "Although – a – a boy would be preferable."
Katherine breathed a laugh at her young husband's excitement and boyish inability to hide his true thoughts.

"Then – if God wills it – a boy it shall be," she said, yet naïve enough to sound confident.

The nausea would not stop, and neither would the eerie cries.
Her head had begun to pound with the ethereal sound reverberating in her head each day, and she could not even find peace in her sleep, for images of her stillborn daughter would haunt her dreams.
The wails were worse during this pregnancy, Katherine realised. Much worse.
They came more often and were more persistent, and there was no avoiding or ignoring them.
But one thing was for sure: the screams she had heard *then* had not been her daughter's…for she had not been granted the gift of her first breath.
With that realisation, however, came another; a much more terrifying possibility: Were the echoing cries that plagued her that of this new babe in her belly?
She shook her head at the thought whenever it crept in. The idea was ludicrous. To believe in such things was preposterous.
And yet…there was no other explanation.
There were no babies at court.

Between the vomiting, lethargy, and the resounding cries that troubled her, Katherine had little time for queenly duties, and she had been rendered bedridden for most of the month of June.

In that time, King Henry's previous discomfort to his privates had returned, his lack of sexual release since the queen's announcement of her condition having left him growing restless once again.

"It has returned," the king informed his physician one day, when the ache was becoming unbearable.

The old man did not ask the king to strip down this time, already knowing what the cause of his discomfort would be.

"Take a mistress, my king," the physician advised yet again, "It is natural for kings to do so when their queen is with child."

A corner of Henry's mouth twitched, he did not enjoy the idea of another woman sharing his bed while his beloved Katherine was bedridden and ill.

"My father never took a mistress," Henry said thoughtfully, "He loved my mother. He also knew that to sire bastards could one day be detrimental to his heir's reign – my reign – in the form of potential usurpers."

The physician nodded slowly, his back hunched slightly with age, "Take a mistress, my king," he repeated nonchalantly, "You father was a clever man, but you needn't worry yourself with your predecessor's concerns. He had obtained a fragile and broken country, and he was not a well-liked man."

The king narrowed his eyes at the older man then, a warning not to slander the monarchy, no matter how accurate the remark may be.

The physician smiled slowly but continued, not fearful to speak the truth, "Your father's concerns of a usurper stemmed from his knowledge that he had not been a popular king. But *you*, your highness, you everyone adores. The country was overjoyed to have you for their king," he shrugged then, as if he didn't care either way, "Father some bastards, what does it matter? Once your queen has given you legitimate sons, the illegitimate ones you may produce along the way will be of no consequence."

Henry swallowed, unsure of what to do with this new outlook. The old man's words rang true, any bastards he may produce would hold no power within England while he and his queen were loved. And they were. The whole country had been overjoyed at their union and had shared their suffering when their princess had been born sleeping.

Perhaps it was not such a terrible idea to bed another woman – only to relieve himself from this discomfort. After all, it was doctor recommended that he do so…

But then he shook his head and exited the old man's chambers. Henry didn't like the idea of betraying his most beloved. And as king he didn't have to do anything he didn't want to do; however harmless the outcome may be.

And he didn't *want* to take a mistress…

Did he?

A week later, the ache in his groin was becoming unbearable. And so were the constant urges.

Women, women, women.

Now that he was toying with the idea of a mistress, women were suddenly all Henry could see.

There were tall ones, short ones, plain ones, beautiful ones. Married or unmarried… there were so many to choose from.

Though he had had many women before marrying Katherine, since their union before God, Henry had not cared for the touch of another, other than his wife.

Being with her had felt different, more soulful, and he had been content in the belief that she would henceforth be his only.

But – as a good wife ought to be – Katherine was proving to be extremely fertile, and she had been pregnant for more months since their marriage than not.

Would Henry really have to spend his life satisfied with just two or three months per year that he could fornicate?

During council meetings he would listen half-heartedly, and in more recent days, Henry forfeited his outdoor activities in exchange for pondering the idea of a lover.

During banquets, the king would observe the people of the court from the top table, where he would often sit alone of late since Katherine continued unwell. And there he would watch the ladies dance, laugh, and sing, and he would consider them – one by one – in an effort to gauge which would be worthy to take to his royal bed.

July 1510

"Anne, the Lady Hastings?" Charles Brandon asked his friend William Compton in a rash whisper one day during a spot of archery.

It was a glorious day. The sun was shining and there was a faint breeze in the air strong enough to keep the men cool, but mild enough to allow a clear shot of the target in the distance. William Compton nodded in confirmation before letting loose of his arrow.

The observers clapped, the arrow having hit just outside of the bull's eye.

"You are playing with fire, William," Charles remarked under his breath, so that their conversation would remain out of the observing courtier's earshot, who stood some feet away, "She is married *and* the sister of the Duke of Buckingham, the king's own cousin! It is in poor taste."

King Henry laughed loudly then, "I think he is well aware of who she is, Charles."

The Lady Anne Hastings had been a lady-in-waiting to Queen Katherine since shortly after their coronation. She had been suggested for the position by Henry himself, since she was of noble birth as a descendant of Edward IV and Elizabeth Woodville – Henry's own grandparents – and married to Lord George Stafford who was a close friend of the king.

William Compton smiled shyly and shook his head at Charles before casting a quick glance at Henry.

The king raised one red eyebrow in silent response.

"As lady-in-waiting to the queen and first cousin to the king himself," Charles said, continuing to note his distaste for Compton's choice of mistress, "Do you not think it disrespectful?"

"To whom? Her husband?" Henry laughed, before clapping Compton on the shoulder.

"No, Henry. To you. To the monarchy," Charles said, loyal as ever to his king.

Henry and William exchanged a look, "I am not offended," the king replied with a casual shrug of his shoulders.

Charles raised his thick, chestnut eyebrows, "No?"

Henry shrugged again, "the Lady Anne Hastings is a fine woman," he said with a hint of indifference, "If she wishes to find solace from her loveless marriage in the arms of another, it is her business."

Charles flashed William a look, which the latter evaded suspiciously, and Charles returned his attention to Henry.

"Of course, your highness," Charles said, before taking his shot at the target, and dropping the subject.

"Scandalous," Katherine's lady-in-waiting, Agnes, summarised after telling her queen the latest court gossip.

The queen could hardly believe it. Her own lady!

Henry's friend William Compton, who Katherine had always believed to be such a kind and graceful gentleman, was being accused of entering into an adulterous affair with one of her own ladies – and not to mention, the king's own cousin – the Lady Anne Hastings.

Katherine frowned in disapproval of the news.

"He may be my lord husband's friend and gentleman of the Privy Council, but that is not the kind of court the king and I wish to govern."

Agnes crossed herself as she shook her head in agreement with her mistress.

"Will you speak to her, Your Grace?" Catalina asked Katherine as she brought her a tray of food, "You must guide her back to God."

Katherine nodded thoughtfully, "She does need guidance back to God, that much is clear. But in this kind of situation, I believe it would be best to inform her lord husband. Let him deal with this in-house, rather than aggravate the scandal further by my involvement."

August 1510

Katherine had begun to feel better just in time for the court's departure from London to the country to avoid the plague.
Her nausea had finally subsided, which she was thankful for now that she was being rocked to-and-fro in the royal carriage during the trip.
Henry had decided to travel only on horseback this time, choosing not to share the royal carriage with his queen, in order to give her more space to be comfortable – this pregnancy having been most unpleasant for the queen.

"You will be more at ease, my love, without my long frame taking up the precious space," Henry had said with a smile before pecking her swiftly on the lips before their departure.
Katherine had smiled back, her heart fluttering with gratitude for her considerate husband.
But now, as they travelled along the dirt path surrounded by fields and trees, Katherine couldn't help but wonder if perhaps the king was trying to distance himself from having to be near her scandalous lady-in-waiting, who continued within the queen's household for the foreceable future.
The queen had informed Anne Hastings' lord husband of the gossip surrounding his wife, for it was only right that her spouse know what the court was whispering so fiercely about.

For the lady's good name and honour was being questioned, and Katherine had to try to save her from herself.

Perhaps she should have insisted she be removed from her household immediately? But then that might have caused more trouble for the lady.

No, it would be best this way.

Let the lady carry on none the wiser until her husband arrives at court to deal with the situation. It would be better for her and Compton if the affair was broken off quietly and without fuss.

"How do you feel, Your Grace?" the Lady Hastings said then, breaking the silence, and Katherine flinched to think she had voiced her thoughts aloud.

The queen cleared her throat, "I am well. Grateful to be past the middle point of our journey."

"Yes," Anne Hastings replied before turning her head to look out the window.

Katherine watched her for a moment. The Lady Anne Hastings had always received much male attention from the gentlemen of the court, her high forehead and small mouth being very favourable to the opposite sex. But Katherine had never thought her to have been the type to be disloyal to her husband…it would certainly have deterred the queen from accepting her as her lady-in-waiting had she known this would come to pass.

Katherine sighed heavily and tore her eyes away from her lady.

The silence that followed felt so heavy and strange that Katherine couldn't help but glance at Catalina beside her, a question in her eyes.

But Catalina only frowned back briefly, unsure of what the queen hoped to convey with no more than a look.

Katherine raised her eyebrows and without moving her head glanced over at Anne who sat before her, still looking out the window.

Catalina followed her gaze cautiously and then nodded at her queen, believing her to be asking for news on the lady's affair. Catalina, knowing only as much as the queen herself, shrugged in response, then nudged her head forwards as if to say, *Perhaps when we arrive.*
Katherine exhaled and nodded slowly, hoping that her Moorish lady would be correct, and that Lord George Hastings would make a swift appearance at the court's first stop in Hampshire so that this debacle could soon be put to bed.

Southwick Priory, Hampshire

The royal progress arrived at the Southwick monastery in Hampshire, where they would reside for the following few days, feeling exhausted and aching all over from the long hours sitting on horseback and in carriages.
Katherine stepped out of her royal carriage slowly, aided by Henry himself who had swiftly swung from his horse to offer his queen a hand as she exited the cramped wagon.
"My queen," Henry said with a wide, flirtatious grin, to which Katherine smiled and averted her gaze shyly.
To think that her handsome husband could still make her feel giddy after almost two years of marriage; it was the stuff of romantic tales. And Katherine was living it.
The royal court made their way into the monastery, all of them in awe of its sacred beauty, despite most of them having seen it on previous progresses before. But its gorgeous architecture never failed to impress them.
While the many horses were being relieved of their wagons and saddles and brought to their stables, the royal court began to settle into their temporary lodgings, the queen being brought to her chamber and fussed over extensively, while the servants prepared for the evening banquet.

"Fetch me some warm water, Anne," Katherine ordered, hoping to be free of the lady for a moment, her dishonour making the queen feel uncomfortable to be around.

The Lady Anne curtsied and left, taking a pitcher with her to fill.

Once she left, Katherine was finally able to exhale the breath she felt she had been holding throughout the whole journey.

"I pray her lord husband will come soon," the queen said, "Or at least that he writes to inform me of what he wishes to do. If he does not wish to travel, then I shall have to speak to her and end this shameful business."

"Do not allow it to fluster you," Catalina said, "You have done a good deed by informing Lord Hastings. He will know what to do."

Katherine sighed, "Even Henry feels it, the shame she exudes. We do not wish to be surrounded by it."

Catalina nodded slowly as she lay another log upon the fire to warm the queen's chambers before she would have to be changed for the banquet.

Anne, the Lady Hastings, was making her way through the unfamiliar corridors and down to the kitchens to fetch the queen's boiled water.

She noticed that, as in the royal palaces, the closer one got to the servants' quarters and the kitchens, the fewer courtiers were about, and it always soothed Anne to know she would find some quiet on her way, even if only for a moment.

As she turned the corner into the dimly lit hallway that would lead to the final staircase to the kitchens, she was not surprised when it appeared to be completely empty.

But as she continued to walk, she noticed two gentlemen were making their way towards her in the shadows.

She kept her head down and the pitcher in her hands as the echoing *clicks* of their heels grew louder as they approached,

their cheerful chatter and laughter reverberating off the stone walls.
And suddenly she knew one of the voices. She knew it from his laugh and from his easy charm.
It was the man she was lucky enough to call her lover.
Just as the two men crossed paths with her, she looked up to meet his gaze, which she had felt on her from a distance.
Their eyes locked for just an instance, his look conveying to her in that brief moment the desire he felt for her.
And then they were past her, their strides never slowing as they went. And as Anne returned her mind to the task ahead, her head swimming with the anticipation of meeting him again later that night, she heard the king's laughter in the growing distance between them, followed by a string of words that she could not make out. And yet she could hear from the tone of his voice that whatever he had said to his friend, William Compton, it had been laden with praise.

Later that evening, Katherine and Henry sat side-by-side overlooking the dozens of courtiers as they feasted merrily.
The royal couple was happy to sit in silence, their love having developed into one that did not need to be filled with constant trivial commentary. And Katherine was grateful for it tonight, for – though her nausea had died down – she was utterly exhausted by the travel and the pregnancy, never mind the chaos within her own household which she felt compelled to resolve.
As the music flowed as constantly as the wine, Katherine felt content.
The incessant cries of the mysterious infant had ceased to echo in her mind some days prior, and it had led the queen to believe that it must have been no more than her worry reshaping itself somehow in the form of those desperate little wails.

But Katherine had felt her baby move inside her belly for the first time some days ago – the first quickenings – which proved that she was indeed with child.

Her peaceful moment was suddenly disrupted then when she saw, from the corner of her eye, the Lady Anne Hastings rising from her seat.

Katherine cast her eyes over the many courtiers in the hall in search of William Compton and saw him then, quite brazenly, leaning against the wall by the great wooden doors at the end of the hall.

Katherine looked to Henry beside her, to see if he had noticed them and to gauge what his reaction was to this shameless scandal occurring right before their very eyes.

But Henry seemed oblivious to it, laughing loudly at something Thomas Wolsey had said beside him.

Katherine was about to turn her gaze away from her husband and back at the two lovers as they approached one another, when suddenly and ever so swiftly, Henry glanced towards the doors where Compton stood.

A look came over Henry's face, one so subtle she might have missed it were she not his wife, but it was there nonetheless: a dark look in his pale blue eyes, his smile vanishing for just a moment, before returning his attention back to Wolsey.

Katherine sighed.

It upset her to see Henry so disappointed in his friend, William Compton. And yet she could not understand why he would not simply discourage Compton from this…

She shook her head and opened her mouth to inform her lord husband that she would retire then, when all of a sudden Henry turned to her, took her hand in his and raised it to his lips.

He kissed her knuckles, "I shall retire," he informed her with a grin, "But stay if you wish. Enjoy the music and the dancing, my love. I shall see you on the morrow."

And with that, the king rose from his seat and hurried towards the doors where, moments ago, Compton had stood awaiting his lady love.

Katherine watched her husband leaving the hall in a hurry, waving away Wolsey and a guard who had followed.

And then, for the slightest of moments and for a reason she could not understand, Katherine's nausea returned.

The following morning, just as the servants had removed the breakfast plates from before Katherine and Henry, the king's usher stood in the doorway, stiff as a statue.

"The Lord George Hastings, your highnesses," he called before returning to his position outside the doors.

Katherine exhaled with relief at the man's arrival. Soon, this scandal would come to an end.

"Lord Hastings?" Henry asked as he frowned at his queen, "What has brought him to my court?"

Katherine smiled at her husband and reached her hand to cover his, glad to finally be able to tell him that he must no longer worry, for she had dealt with the matter.

"I summoned him here," she admitted proudly.

Henry's frown deepened, which Katherine could not understand.

"Whatever for?!" he asked harshly, tearing his hand from hers.

Katherine flinched. Never had Henry spoken to her in such a tone, nor would she have guessed that he would show anything but relief or gratitude to what she had done.

His reaction nicked her like the tip of a sharp knife.

"I know he is your friend, my lord," Katherine said as she tried to reach for his hand once more, "But I thought you too were irked by Compton's involvement in the Lady Hastings' adultery."

It was Henry's turn to flinch, but he did not reply.

Instead, he exhaled angrily and rose so abruptly from his seat that it scrapped against the stone floor, and he headed for the door.

Katherine stared after him, her mouth hanging open as she failed to comprehend her husband's reaction.

The queen followed her king to receive Lord Hastings, though she was unable to keep up with his long strides fuelled by anger. She eventually found them in the hall, Henry sitting on his throne at the far end and Hastings bowing in greeting before his monarch.

As Katherine approached with her ladies in tow, stunned with her lord husband for having hurried off and left her behind, she could tell from the creased expression on both the men's faces that there was tension in the air.

Katherine had been prepared for Lord Hastings to be upset and disappointed, of course.

What she *hadn't* expected, was her own husband's disgruntled response.

Lord Hastings bowed to his queen as she took her seat on the throne beside the king's, her ladies – including the Lady Hastings – standing obediently beside Katherine, and before she had even gotten her swollen body comfortable, the man began rambling about the issue.

In front of everyone.

"I received word from Your Grace, my queen, that I should come at once to address the matter at hand regarding my wife. The gossip that surrounds her is a disgrace and I am appalled to find out –"

Katherine's ears began ringing then as her heart beat rapidly in her chest. She cast her eyes over the many courtiers dotted around in the hall who had been engrossed in their conversations or games of cards.

But at the man's ranting they were no longer absorbed in their activities, and all were now looking in their direction.

She *had* hoped to avoid this public discussion of her lady's offence against her lord husband.
It was precisely why she had summoned the man here, so that they may speak privately, rather than Katherine addressing the matter herself and making it a public issue.
But now it had most certainly become a public issue.
Katherine glanced over at Anne Hastings, feeling terrible for her part in this public berating.

"My Lord," Henry called then, interrupting the man's stream of words, "I understand your disappointment. You have been cuckolded and it is a shambles. But what do you wish for *me* to do about it? You are the Lady Hastings' lord husband."

"But...Your Grace, it is *your* close friend who has committed the offence against me!" Lord Hastings replied.
Katherine's cheeks burned brightly as she watched the discussion unfold before dozens of courtiers, all of them staring up at the Lady Hastings beside her.
Some even glancing sheepishly at Katherine herself.
She hung her head in shame at having called Lord Hastings to court. It might have been less of a public debacle had she simply spoken to Henry herself.
After all, the Lady Hastings was the kings' own cousin. Surely, he would have been lenient on her.
She sighed at her naivety.

An agreement was made to settle the scandal.
William Compton was commanded to take the sacrament swearing that he had not had his way with Lord George's wife.
And Anne Hastings, at the mercy of her husband, was banished from court and sent to a nunnery where she would reside for the foreseeable future to atone for her sins.

"This was none of your concern, Katherine!" the king bellowed at his wife later that day after a tense and uncomfortable banquet.

They were in the queen's chambers, alone save for Katherine's remaining two ladies, Agnes and Catalina.

She glanced at them then wide-eyed, so surprised was she by Henry's outburst that Katherine needed confirmation from their reactions that she was not being overly sensitive.

But, strangely, they both hung their heads and hurried out the door.

It would seem Katherine was indeed in the wrong.

"Henry," Katherine said, hoping to explain herself, "I could tell that their affair was causing you great unease. I had hoped that Lord Hastings would have been discreet in the handling of the matter, perhaps even in such a way that he would have needed no more than our permission to remove Anne from my household in favour of the nunnery. I did not for a moment believe him to be so outspoken about it! At the very least to preserve his own reputation, if not his wife's."

Henry had moved away from her as she had spoken, raking a hand through his thick, coppery hair in frustration.

Katherine scoffed in confusion and shook her head at her husband.

But then irritation began to overcome her as Henry continued so oddly perturbed since learning of Lord Hasting's summons.

From the very start, Henry could have avoided this simply by ordering his friend William to stop pursuing the Lady Anne.

If he, as king, had not condoned their adultery, then why had he not intervened –?

The reality of it all hit Katherine suddenly then.

It hit her like a blow to the gut.

"You were accepting of it all along…"

Henry turned to look at her then, a pained expression in his eyes, which led Katherine to an even deeper confusion still, despite having finally understood the situation a little better.

"Why do you look at me so?" Katherine whispered, feeling suddenly quite hot.

Henry's face crumpled, his eyebrows etched together with angst as he turned away from her and shook his head, his hands on either side of his head.

It was in that moment that Katherine knew why he looked suddenly so forlorn.

Because she had asked all the right questions, and yet his reactions had made no sense.

Katherine's chest felt heavy then as all the pieces fell into place, and she clenched her jaw together tightly, as though to let herself relax would cause her to crumble.

"It was you," she whispered breathlessly, "It was you who was having an affair with Anne."

It all *finally* made sense.

The brief dark look that had crossed over Henry's face as he had spotted Compton and the lady by the doors of the hall last night. It had not been a look of disapproval after all. But a look of...anticipation?

Had Anne and Henry met up last night when he had left the banquet so swiftly? With Compton as the intermediary? The cover?

Other moments came suddenly to mind, each of them like stab wounds to the heart.

The courtiers looking up at Anne in horror during her husband's public ranting, while others looked at Katherine with what she had thought was disappointment at her involvement. But had they actually been looks of...*pity?*

Henry choosing to ride horseback on the long journey to Hampshire rather than sharing a carriage with his wife and her ladies. It had not been to give his expecting wife more space, nor had it been because he had felt uncomfortable to be around the adulterous Lady Hastings…

But because he would have been seated for hours between his queen and his whore.

Katherine felt suddenly lightheaded, and she pressed a hand to her clammy forehead.

How could she have missed it?

How did she not *see?*

She had believed Henry would remain faithful while she was with child…

She had been naïve.

And Henry…Henry had been a liar.

"Katherine," Henry mumbled pathetically then as he moved towards her, his hands reaching out to aid her into a seat as she wobbled unsteadily on her feet.

But she slapped the king's hand away, an action which might have been punishable by death in different circumstances.

But in that moment, she did not even care.

"Do not touch me!" the queen hollered as she lowered herself onto the chair by the fire, which she wished then was not roaring so brightly, for the realisation of her husband's infidelity was causing her head to ache and her vision to blur.

"I never meant for you to find out," Henry mumbled as he tried to reach for her hand, completely dismissing her wish not to be touched.

His words sliced her like a knife, another scar to add to the many his infidelity had inflicted.

I never meant for you to find out…

It did not suggest regret that he had betrayed her, only that he had been caught.

Katherine sat there in silence, staring at a smudge of black ash in the fireplace.

"Why?" she asked finally, her voice low, for she had no more energy left for this wicked betrayal.

Henry *tutted* then and turned away from her, beginning to pace, "You are with child, Katherine!" he exclaimed, as though this whole ordeal were somehow her doing, "I cannot lay with you and – my balls *hurt*! They ache *all the time*! Do you know how uncomfortable that is?"

His eyes were pleading for her to understand, as though creating and birthing a child was an easy task in comparison to his aching privates.

The queen stared up at Henry, her eyes so wide she feared they might pop from their sockets. She could not believe her ears.

Her young husband. Her young, *stupid* husband.

He would not have lasted a day in a woman's body.

And yet, he went on.

"The physicians told me to take a mistress. And I didn't want to. I swear it, Katherine, I didn't intend to. But –" and he stood before her, his fingers curled in frustration, "They *hurt*!"

Katherine looked down at her husband's codpiece as it poked out of his hose as was fashionable, and she felt a sudden gush of disgust coarse through her to think of him inside another woman – but more disgusted still by his form of explanation of his discomforts.

She looked away from him.

There was no more she could say or do.

The betrayal was done and – though unwittingly – Katherine has had his mistress removed from court.

"Do not think to take another," the queen finally said, her tone purposefully low so that he had to lean forward to hear.

She wanted to remind him that, though he was her husband and king, she too held some power. Even if only in his still young and impressionable mind.

Henry's jaw ticked at her words. He did not enjoy the insinuation of an order, however slight, and Katherine worried for a moment if she was beginning to lose his admiration.

They stared each other down for a moment, neither of them willing to be the first to speak, and Katherine knew that if she weren't with child, this tension would have been extinguished in the bedroom.

And yet, if I wasn't with child, this entire situation would never have happened in the first place.

At the thought, the queen tore her eyes from the king.

She could not even blame him.

This was the way of things.

She was doing her duty by bearing her king children, and the reality of it was that he would need another plaything to keep him satisfied while she could not lay with him.

But the idea of Anne Hastings or any other woman sleeping with her beloved husband made her shiver with hatred.

Katherine might never like it – sharing him with his whores – but she realised it was not realistic to believe him to remain faithful.

She would have to allow it…

As long as Henry made sure to remember who his queen was.

Chapter 10

August 1510

The construction of the two new warships designed and approved earlier in the year were to commence.
The larger of the two – and Henry's favourite – was to be named Mary Rose – Mary, after the Virgin Mary, and Rose to signify the Tudor emblem.
The Mary Rose would be the one to carry the eight large guns, and she would be the largest ship in the English navy.
Her smaller sister – though she too would be a warship – would not carry guns or be as grand as the Mary Rose, and she was named Peter Pomegranate, after St Peter and the queen's symbol of the Pomegranate.
King Henry was as giddy as a young boy as constructions began, his vision of a strong and fighting-fit England taking form right before his eyes and at his own design.

"With the English navy strengthening and the queen's belly growing daily, soon we will be in a good position to wage war on France," Henry said gleefully, his eyes shining with a hope only ever seen in the young.

Thomas Wolsey, who continued on the rise in the king's good graces, nodded his head.

"It certainly sends a message to our European rivals that England is not to be underestimated," Wolsey agreed.

"Good!" Henry exclaimed with a grin, flashing his straight white teeth, and he clapped Wolsey on the shoulder, "Gone are the days of penny-pinching as my father did before me. What use is all my money if I don't use it to England's advantages?"

Wolsey smiled, "You are a good king," he said, "I trust you shall lead the country to a much brighter future."

November 1510

The queen was believed to be about seven months into her pregnancy according to the physicians. But they were unaware of the king and queen's secret coupling during her last confinement.
Which was why, when the queen's bump had grown larger than the physicians believed she ought to be, they – once again – gave their expert opinion that Katherine must be carrying twins.

"Twins!" Henry said, his blue eyes wide and shining with joy, "What splendid news, my love!"
He had reached for her hand and Katherine had reluctantly allowed him to take it, for she still continued vexed by his betrayal with Anne Hastings.

"How can they be sure?" Katherine replied, unwilling to fall for the physician's educated guesses. Then she leaned forward, "I may simply be further along."
Henry's mouth twitched into a mischievous, lopsided grin, still bashful at the mention of their forbidden lovemaking.

"I personally wish for twins, don't you?" the king replied as he sipped his wine, "Ha! How splendid that would be!"
Katherine smiled faintly, but it did not reach her eyes, for she cared little as to whether there be one or five babies in her belly. All she cared about was that they would live.
Henry raised her hand to his lips, "Fear not, my love," he said as he kissed her knuckles, "Tragedy is surely behind us."
The queen met his hopeful eyes and nodded.
Then Henry smiled, hoping to move past the gloomy reminder of their daughter's death.

"Your confinement will commence soon. And before you are to be hidden away from me once more, I have arranged for many wonderful entertainments to lift your spirits."

Katherine frowned briefly, wondering what he had planned, but she could not help but smile at her husband's good-naturedness.

It was almost enough for her to forget his adultery.

But not quite.

For the following days the English court was alive with festivities.

The king himself partook in a magnificent joust, outshining all other participants with his skill and grandeur.

This was followed by a grand banquet comprising of hundreds of rich and extravagant foods and wine, which the court feasted on merrily.

Dances and plays were performed, as well as a particularly splendorous performance where Henry and fifteen gentlemen pranced in front of Katherine and the audience in fanciful costumes.

They danced before the queen wearing jackets of purple and crimson with white velvet bonnets, capped with white plumes, and after the dancing they exited and returned moments later, masked, and wearing yellow satin and carrying torches.

Ladies suddenly emerged from among the audience dressed in crimson satin gowns, embroidered with pomegranates made of cloth of gold.

The ladies danced with the gentlemen, all of which – including the audience – pretended not to know which of the masked gentlemen was the king – though he was the tallest, leanest man among them.

Once the dance was concluded, the ladies removed the men's masks and all those in attendance cheered to identify the young and handsome king as he stared, grinning, at his beloved queen at the front of the audience.

Katherine had returned his intense gaze, her mouth curved into a pretty smile as she wordlessly thanked him for the thoughtful festivities with a lustful look.

The king inhaled and puffed out his chest slightly to see her look at him so.

He had achieved his desired goal, and he could tell simply from the look in Katherine's eyes that if she were not heavy with child, that she would be leading him to her bedchambers this instant.

With these elaborate performances of chivalry and courtly love, Henry had wished to gain her forgiveness for straying. And it seemed his wooing was beginning to work.

December 1510
Richmond Palace, Surrey

The Christmastide was approaching, but Katherine would not be around to partake in the festivities, for she was to enter her confinement.

On the day before she would retire to the gloomy and stuffy chambers for the following few weeks, the queen heard mass and then hosted a banquet for all the men and women of the court in her great chamber.

In honour of Christmas, spiced wine flowed freely all night, the courtiers laughing merrily as the night went on in a flurry of upbeat music and cheerful dancing.

"May I walk you to your confinement chambers later?" Henry asked quietly as he leaned closer to his wife halfway through the evening, the court laughing and talking gaily before them.

Katherine could smell the spiced wine on his breath, and it made her feel dizzy. She nodded her head once, lightheaded from the way that he looked at her now, just moments before they would be parted for weeks until their baby was born.

At midnight, the royal couple withdrew themselves quietly from the court and made their way up the wide staircase and through the candle-lit hallways.

They stopped short at the threshold to the birthing chamber, where men were traditionally not allowed entrance to – though they both knew Henry had disregarded that rule once before.

"You look radiant," Henry said as he smiled down at her.

Katherine averted her gaze, "If I do it is thanks to you."

Henry lifted her chin with his finger gently and made her meet his eyes, "All will be well," he whispered to her, his eyes no longer shining with overbearing arrogance but with a certainty that Katherine hoped was contagious.

His conviction relaxed her a little, and she smiled up at him briefly.

Henry bent his head then to kiss her, a kiss both firm and gentle all at once.

His finger remained under her chin, then trailed down her neck slowly as their lips remained locked.

A shiver of desire rushed through Katherine at his touch, and she released a low moan.

The king broke away from his queen then, his eyelids heavy as he looked down at her passionately.

"You will not take another mistress while I am in confinement, will you?"

The words fell out of Katherine's mouth before she knew she had been thinking them, and for a brief moment, her eyes widened with surprise at herself and the brazenness of her question.

Henry breathed a laugh, but his pale blue eyes never strayed from hers as he replied, "No. I do not intend to ever take another."

Katherine exhaled, relieved.

But she pressed her luck, "Do you promise?"

And then there it was. Ever so brief but very much present, nonetheless.

The beat of hesitation that Katherine had feared.

"I promise."

Two weeks into the queen's confinement, the echoing wails of a baby returned to haunt Katherine's already anxious mind. She had thought them to be a thing of the past when she had been relieved from them for several weeks; but now her subconscious was taunting her once more, the babe's desperate cries becoming more and more heart wrenching with each day that passed.

The birthing chambers were dark and dismal, heavy tapestries having been hung over the windows to achieve the womb-like state the midwives believed was necessary for the safe arrival of the baby. Only one window was to be opened from time to time to allow for some semblance of fresh air to enter – but even that remained shuttered for most of the day.

To pass the time in these dark and dreary days, Katherine took herself to her private prie-deux in the corner of the chambers for hours each day, hoping to alleviate the distant wailing in her subconscious and to pray to God that He would clear her mind of fear and worry.

But He did not.

And each morning she would awake to the agonising crying of a baby that was not really there...

Until one evening, on the 31st of December, the queen began to feel the familiar pinch that meant the beginnings of labour, and it suddenly occurred to her that perhaps the cries were not her mind's way of showcasing her fear after all...

Perhaps, instead of that...they were a warning.

1st January 1511

  The queen's tightenings had continued all night, growing stronger and closer together with each hour that passed.
The pain was almost unbearable, her entire bump squeezing every few minutes with such a force she felt like she was being ripped in half.
It felt nothing like the last time.
But then again…perhaps that was a good thing.
At around three in the morning, the queen's waters finally broke as she had stood, squatting, at the foot of the pallet bed, the warm, clear liquid gushing down her legs.
  "The time to push is near," one of the queen's midwives said at the breaking of the waters, her cheeks pink with excitement.
But Katherine was not excited.
She was absolutely terrified.
An hour later, the queen's birthing chamber was filled with people, half a dozen midwives scurrying from one side of the room to the other, their white caps and white gowns making it impossible to tell them apart.
As one left the queen's side another would take her place, each one with their own purpose: to bring a new, fresh towel before taking a soiled one away, to wipe the queen's brow, or to raise a cup of small ale to her lips.
It went on and on like that for hours, one midwife replacing another in a constant conveyor belt of childbearing tasks, as Katherine pushed through muffled grunts and gritted teeth.
And then – finally – the sun rose, and the darkness melted away, rays of gold poking over the horizon and through the shuttered windows like tiny beams of life.
It gave Katherine strength, to think of her baby being born with the rising of the sun on New Year's Day. This baby that would surely live and grow up to become a prince or princess of England.

Katherine inhaled deeply as Catalina held her hand beside her, and with one great, final push, Katherine of Aragon gave birth to her baby.

"It is a boy!" the midwife who now held him in her arms called out gleefully.

Then, as soon as the umbilical cord was cut, he let out a strong and healthy newborn wail.

And Katherine could relax, for she had finally found the source of the crying.

Upon his birth, Henry VIII's legitimate son was automatically titled Duke of Cornwall, as the reigning monarch's heir apparent.

The young king had never been so happy. Not even his coronation had given Henry as much joy as the birth of his precious boy had done, and he hurried through the palace ecstatically, telling everyone he passed that his most wonderful wife had borne him a healthy son.

He ordered bonfires to be lit in the streets of London and instructed the Lord Mayor to organize for the citizens to be served free wine to toast to the health of the prince.

And while Henry hurried about, arranging celebrations and prayers, Katherine lay abed, watching from her great four-poster bed as the midwives washed and swaddled her child.

Henry had ordered for an entirely new cradle to be built – the many pieces of furniture built for their previous baby having been destroyed for fear of tempting fate – and as the little prince was gently placed into his newly built cradle, Katherine felt a wave of love flooding her soul.

She had done it. She had done her duty.

And it was more delicious than she had ever imagined it would be, for this baby was suddenly everything.

Immediately upon his birth, it was as though a life without him had never been, for she could hardly even remember the moments, days and years that had come before.

None of them mattered anymore.
This prince was now Katherine's past and her present.
And if God was good, he would be her future.

Chapter 11

2nd January 1511

The following day, when Katherine was well enough to sit up, her bed was moved to the presence chamber where she would receive guests – ladies of the court, duchesses, and wives of the members of the Privy Chamber.
The queen was dressed in a crimson mantle, her newborn son sleeping soundly beside her in his painted wood cradle with silver gilt and buckles on either side to secure the swaddling bands.
The midwives had regarded the boy as completely healthy following their assessment upon his birth and concluded him strong enough for his christening to be deferred to take place in a few days – rather than immediately, as a sickly baby would have been.
It gave Katherine great joy, and she felt elated with pride for what she had created.
She looked down into her son's cradle as he slept, watching the rhythmic up and down of his chest as he breathed, his stumpy little eyelashes moving ever so slightly as he dreamed of – what? What did newborn babies even dream of?
Katherine could not even guess, but she sighed deeply and smiled to herself, utterly besotted with him.
He was his father's mirror image, that much was instantly clear. Though the little baby sported chubby cheeks and a squished-up face – as all newborns did – he had his father's nose as well as his thin lips, and on the top of his head sprouted a little wisp of swirly, bright orange hair.
He was perfect. There was no denying that.
  "Does your majesty wish to rest a while?" Catalina asked in a hushed voice then when the final guest had left.

Katherine nodded and waved her hand for the servants and the baby's wetnurse to wheel the cradle out into the adjoining room.

"How do you feel, Your Grace?" Catalina asked, her dark eyes raking over Katherine protectively.

"I feel tired," the queen said as if in confirmation that all else was well, "Do not fret, Lina. The king was right," and she smiled faintly as she lay her head down on the pillow and closed her eyes to sleep, "All will be well."

Sunday, 5th January 1511
Chapel of the Observant Friars, Richmond, Surrey

A twenty-four-foot-wide walkway was newly gravelled between the palace hall and the chapel in preparation for the prince's christening.

It was then strewn with flowers on the morning of the event, and barriers were erected on either side to keep the excited public from coming too close to the king and queen's precious heir.

The way was hung with rich cloth of arras, and despite the gloomy January weather, the walkway looked sumptuous, colourful, and bright.

The French King Louis de Valois and the Archbishop of Canterbury, William Warham, had been chosen for the prince's godfathers. Katherine of York the Countess of Devon and daughter of Edward IV, as well as Margaret of Austria Duchess of Savoy, for his godmothers.

Vast crowds of people gathered for a glimpse of their new prince, and an excited murmur had begun, like the buzz of a beehive, as they awaited the start of the lavish display.

As the procession began the crowds' hubbub dissipated, their eagerness to gossip blown away with the wind, and the little prince emerged, carried safely in one of his godmother's arms.

Margaret of Austria began her slow walk along the gravelled path towards the chapel, cradling the four-day-old prince as he slept peacefully in her arms, completely unaware of the grand event that was taking place in his honour.

The other prince's godparents followed behind, the Bishop of Winchester appearing as proxy for the French King, who had remained in France but had been good enough to send fine gifts of a gold salt holder and a gold cup, as well as a silver rattle.

The priest was awaiting them at the chapel door and upon their arrival Margaret of Austria presented the prince to him so that he may be blessed.

The priest opened the prince's gummy mouth gently and rubbed salt onto his gums with his wrinkly pinkie finger.

"I hereby exorcise any demons that may prevail onto thee, and bestow upon thee the reception of wisdom," he called, and all the while, the little prince slept.

They entered the church.

Throughout the length of the aisle, on both sides towards the baptismal font, hung beautiful tapestries that had been hand stitched and decorated with pearls and precious stones.

Upon their arrival at the silver font the old priest took his place beside it as the king's chaplain began singing *Te Deum*.

"I ask you, oh Lord," he said above the singing, "to bless this water so that this child may be cleansed of sin," he touched the water with his right hand and completed a prayer over it.

He then, ever so carefully, sprinkled the water over the prince's wispy red curls three times as he said, "I baptize you in the name of the Father, the Son, and the Holy Spirit."

The old priest then turned to the crowd of lords and ladies within the church, and as Margaret of Austria held the prince up high for all to see, he called out, "This child has been reborn in baptism and is now a child of God. He has been

reborn and will forever be known as Henry, his royal highness, Duke of Cornwall, and Prince of England!"
The crowd erupted in cheerful applause and calls of joy, which finally resulted in waking the little prince.
His little face scrunched up in annoyance at the rude awakening before opening his little pink mouth and releasing a high-pitched wail.
The crowd of lords and ladies cooed in unison at the prince's sad little protest and his godmother lay him back down in the safety of her arms and rocked him gently to soothe him.
But the little prince kept on wailing angrily as the crowd continued to mumble gentle sounds of encouragement.
Little did they know that some distance away, Katherine had jolted awake from her rest for a reason unknown to her.
She was too far away from her child – hundreds of meters of space between them – to have heard the people's cheers, nevermind her newborn baby's little cry.
And yet she had heard it. Or rather – *felt* it.
It was a sorrowful resonance she would likely never shake – the echo of her son's wails having embedded themselves into her very soul.

10th January 1511

Baby Hal was nine days old and thriving.
He was a beautiful and peaceful baby, doing little other than sleeping or feeding heartily from his wet nurses' breasts.
As was common practice, Katherine remained in confinement to rest and regain her strength, but also because a woman's bleedings – as well as childbirth itself – was deemed as sinful and unclean, and before she could be readmitted into society Katherine would have to be churched by a priest.
While his family was resting however, King Henry could not sit still.

There was so much to do, so many celebrations to organise and events to be planned in honour of his son's birth.

But above even all that, Henry was in desperate need to give thanks to God for this joyous gift of life.

With a company of a dozen guards, Henry mounted his horse one brisk morning and set off at a gallop, eager to visit the Norfolk shrine of Our Lady at Walsingham.

Walsingham had been a place of pilgrimage for centuries and was one of the four great shrines of Christendom – alongside that of Jerusalem, Rome, and Santiago da Compostella – ever since 1061, when a noble lady had had a series of visions of the Virgin Mary.

In her visions, the Blessed Virgin Mary had fetched the lady's soul during a religious trance from England to a house in Nazareth, where the angel Gabriel had made his revelation of the birth of Jesus. And following the lady's awakening from her trance, her noble family in Walsingham had built a replica of the holy house that she had seen in her visions.

For the centuries to come, Walsingham was visited by thousands of pilgrims from all over England and other European countries, including nearly all the kings and queens of England since Henry III, who had reigned around three hundred years prior.

And Henry VIII would now continue these royal visits, to give thanks to Our Lady for the safe birth of his son and heir. Upon their arrival at the village, a mile away from the Slipper Chapel, Henry dismounted his great horse and removed his shoes.

"I shall proceed barefoot," the king announced, to which the guards looked at one another but said nothing as they too dismounted their horses but did not remove their shoes.

Once Henry arrived at the chapel, he lit a candle and made an offering of expensive jewels – rubies and diamonds – and commissioned the royal glazier, one Barnard Flower, to make a stained-glass window for the chapel.

Henry believed this would be enough to show God how thankful he was for this blessing of a son, and when the sun was beginning to set on the horizon, the king and his guards mounted their horses, and returned to their queen.

30th January 1511

Queen Katherine had recuperated swiftly, and arrangements were made for the court to return to Westminster Palace.
Once the queen had been purified in the churching ceremony and deemed fit to return to society, she emerged from the birthing chambers to a fanfare of applauding courtiers, her husband at the very heart of the praising crowd.

"I have never been as joyous as I am this day where you are returned to me," Henry said as he took her hand and kissed it before kneeling before her, like a knight to his fair maiden.

The crowd mumbled in surprised awe to see the king bend his knee to anyone, many of the court ladies swooning at the public display of love and respect.

"You have given me the most precious gift," the king concluded as he looked up at her.

"I have done no more than my duty," Katherine replied humbly, though a great smile brightened her face.

As was tradition, the prince would be separated from his parents and remain at his nursery at Richmond, to be cared for by his governess, wet nurses, and rockers.

His royal parents would visit whenever possible, but the prince's daily regime would be overseen by his governess.

It ached Katherine's heart to be parted from her son, her baby that had been a part of her for the past nine months and that would suddenly be out of reach, many miles away.

But it was the way of things. Royal babies were not their parent's, but the country's, and for baby Hal to have the best possible future, Katherine knew she had to let him go.

Chapter 12

3rd February 1511
Westminster Palace, London

Once the royal court had returned to Westminster, the lavish events the king had organised to celebrate the birth of his heir and the glorious queen who had birthed him, were able to commence.
Though she and her ladies had been kept in the dark as to the details of the entertainments, the court was oozing with excitement for what was to come.
One morning, as Katherine was breakfasting with her sister-in-law Mary, the ladies were interrupted by a handful of costumed courtiers.

"Will Your Graces please follow us?" the one at the lead said, extending his hand for the queen to take. Katherine looked over at Mary – now a beautiful young princess of fifteen-years-old with hair the colour of the dawn – who shrugged her delicate shoulders.
They were led to the jousting tiltyard at the bottom of the field behind the palace.

"It will be a joust, no doubt," her lady Catalina said to Agnes as they walked behind Katherine and Mary.

"But the costumed chaperones," Agnes pointed out, "Perhaps it is a play."
Katherine smiled to hear that her ladies were as clueless as she, though she too believed Henry had organised for a splendid joust to take place – his favourite sporting event.
When they arrived at the tiltyard however, she had not been prepared for what they would encounter, and she was dazzled to find the whole area decorated entirely like a forest, complete with rocks, trees, ferns, grass, and even hills and valleys.

They stepped into the makeshift forest, Katherine's mouth hanging agape as she looked about in wonder.

Despite its luscious decoration, the tiltyard appeared completely empty as they made their way through the magical makeshift forest and up the steps to her throne.

Katherine and Mary took their seat slowly, hyper-vigilant to anything that could jump out at them to commence the event. Suddenly six men appeared dressed as hermits and pilgrims and Mary giggled beside her and pointed excitedly at one of them, "That is most certainly Charles Brandon!"

They blew their horns upon gathering before their smiling queen and princess, and at the sound four knights appeared from among the trees, one of whom Katherine recognised immediately as her lord husband, for she would recognise his athletic build anywhere.

She grinned cheerfully as she spotted him, her love, and as he led his armed knights towards her, Katherine could see that something was embroidered onto his riding skirt.

She narrowed her eyes to read it, but he was moving too much, his horse having been brought to him then to commence the pageant.

"What does that read, Mary?" Katherine asked, but Mary too did not see it well enough, the young princess' attention being fixed on the pilgrim she believed to be Charles in disguise.

But then one of the disguised knights – Henry – swung himself expertly on his horse and steered it towards his queen, the horns still blowing a fanfare in the background, and on the steed's trapper, those same words as on the king's skirt were embroidered.

"*Cure loial,*" Katherine read under her breath, *Loyal Heart.* Her heart burst with love for her handsome husband then as she realised his grand profession of love for her.

"My queen," Henry now said before her as he held his long lance under one of his arms and reached it towards her, "Will you grant me the gift of your favour?"

Katherine's cheeks flushed with adoration as her ladies and Mary giggled beside her, and she averted her gaze briefly like a love-sick girl. Then she stood from her throne and walked towards the edge of the rafters before reaching into the top of her corseted dress and pulling out her personal handkerchief from between her breasts. It was embroidered at the corner with a gold-stitched 'K' and a pomegranate – her symbol.

"For luck, Sir Loyal Heart," she called to him as she tied the handkerchief around the end of the knight's lance.

Beneath his mask, Katherine could tell that Henry was grinning up at her in that lopsided, toothy grin Katherine loved so much.

"I do not need luck," Henry replied mischievously before steering his horse around to take his place.

By now, the makeshift forest was filled with many lords and ladies of the court, all of them having been invited to join and observe the magnificent contest, and as they stood watching from all around, the king and his knights began to joust.

The joust continued for many rounds, the sound of applause and cheering continuing throughout, and the king partook in twenty-five rounds – more than any of the other riders. Katherine took this to mean that he was clearly in high spirits, and it made her chest soar with pride that she had brought this joy out in him.

Though Henry did not win the tournament he remained cheerful while Katherine bestowed prizes on the champion, and at the end of the event the king showed off his riding skills through a series of acrobatic turns with his horse. The court clapped in awe of their young and capable king, but Henry cared only for his wife's admiration, and when he looked up into the canopy through the cloud of dust he had created, he was glad to see, through the lust in his wife's eyes, that he had achieved it.

For in that moment, though Henry's face was covered in sweat and dirt, to Katherine, he had never looked more handsome.

With the near daily festivities coming to an end, Katherine could no longer wait to pay a visit to her baby Hal.

"I wish to visit our son," Katherine told Henry one morning over a grand breakfast of many extravagant meats and pastries, "I miss him dearly."

Henry looked over at his beautiful wife, "You may of course visit Hal," he said, "In fact, I think I would like to visit him too, to oversee his household is working well in our absence."

Katherine smiled, her stomach flipping with excitement to see her baby boy.

Due to her separation from him, her body had been feeling at a loss lately, as though she were missing a vital limb. It felt entirely unnatural to be away from her baby, though of course she knew never to voice these thoughts.

Their separation had been necessary to allow for a swift conception of a spare heir, which – though she had done her duty by producing Hal – was a woman's primary purpose while she continued in her youth.

But to be granted permission to return to Richmond so soon after their departure was like music to Katherine's ears.

She really was the luckiest woman in all of Europe, to have married the considerate and loving Henry VIII.

21st February 1511
Richmond Palace, London

King Henry and Queen Katherine arrived at Richmond Palace with a small entourage, their visit intended to be but a short one.

As soon as the carriage came to a halt, the royal couple exited excitedly, Katherine practically running up the staircase to the royal nursery.

The guards held open the wooden doors for her as she approached, followed closely by the king who had quickened his pace to catch up with his wife.

"Oh," Katherine breathed as she spotted the cradle at the centre of the room. She approached it like a moth to a flame, almost as though she had no control of her body, and her eyes widened in awe as Hal came into sight and she took in all his perfect little features.

She was vaguely aware of the baby's many wet nurses, rockers and linen washers curtsying at hers and Henry's entrance, but she only had eyes for her son.

Though they had only been parted for three weeks, Katherine could already tell that he had changed significantly: he appeared bigger, his cheeks plumper and pink, like two red apples.

He must be feeding well from his wet nurses, she thought, and a pang of pride squeezed her heart.

But more noticeable of all was the thick tangle of coppery red curls that had blossomed upon his head.

Katherine walked over to the cradle where he slept soundly, his rocker sitting on a seat beside him, swaying the cradle ever so gently.

"He sleeps so peacefully," Katherine remarked as Henry arrived at her side and they both looked down at Hal's chubby face.

Henry wrapped his arm around his wife's waist, "That's because he knows he is loved."

Katherine smiled at Henry's words but did not tear her gaze from her baby's pouty little mouth.

"He is a joy, your highnesses," Hal's governess said then from across the room, "He feeds well and has been no trouble during the night."

Henry nodded at the governess in thanks for the update, then looked back down at his son as the child began to stir awake, his arms raised high above his head and his legs bent up in that newborn scrunch. His little hand nudged the silver rattle at the corner of the cradle, the little toy *jingling* briefly at his touch, and then Hal released a little frustrated squeal, his face squished up angrily at being woken.

"Oh," Katherine cooed as she breathed a laugh, her chest aching with love for her child.

She reached into the cradle and lifted him gently, making sure to support his head.

She placed him in the crook of her arm and then pressed her lips to the top of his head. She inhaled his sweet scent, an aroma so unique to that of a newborn baby it was almost impossible to describe – a mixture of milk and honey, perhaps?

"Oh my goodness, Henry," Katherine said with a great smile as she turned to her husband, "He smells so..." and she sighed, unable to express the love she was feeling for her baby in that moment.

She bent down to retrieve the rattle from the cradle and shook it gently before Hal's angry little face, her heart skipping a beat to see her baby relax at the chiming sound.

"Do you wish to hold him?" Katherine asked Henry then.

The king hesitated, and Katherine was suddenly reminded that Henry had likely never held a newborn baby before.

He had not wanted to hold their stillborn daughter last year; he had said it would have been too hard.

Had he held his sister, Mary, when she had been born? He had only been five years old at the time of her birth...even if he had held her, he likely wouldn't remember.

Katherine smiled reassuringly and took a step towards him; baby Hal having calmed down in his mother's arms.

Henry looked at his son and noticed his pale blue eyes staring back at him, exactly like his own, and he realised that he would like nothing more than to feel the weight of his precious heir in his arms.

"Leave us," Henry ordered, "We wish for a moment alone with our son."

The royal couple watched patiently as the room emptied out, the rocker, wetnurses, servants and guards following the prince's governess out the door.

Once the door to the nursery was closed, Henry led his little family to the loungers by the fire.

Katherine sat down gingerly, her chubby infant hugged closely against her.

He squealed then, pounding his little clenched fists into the air, but Katherine instinctively bounced him and shook the rattle gently to settle him.

"*Shhh,*" she cooed.

Henry sat beside them and watched his beloved wife.

She was a natural mother, he thought. Gentle and calming, but he knew her also to be strong when needed. He knew that she would protect her child fiercely and without question, no matter what.

She reminded him of his own mother then, for she too had been a gentle and calm soul, but with a fire within her where her children's wellbeing was concerned.

"Do you wish to hold him?" Katherine asked again then as she smiled encouragingly at Henry beside her.

His eyes flashed briefly with uncertainty as he looked down at the fragile little person in her arms, but he nodded his head once before swallowing his nervousness.

The king reached out his arms as Katherine adjusted baby Hal in hers, then lifted him over to his father carefully.

Henry licked his dry lips as he gripped his son under his armpits and held him against his chest.

"What now?" Henry asked, his eyes wide as he searched Katherine's face for guidance.

"Hold his head," she instructed, "then lay him down in the crook of your arm –"
Henry had done as she had instructed, he had supported the head and tried to prop Hal into the fold of his arm, but the baby had wriggled in frustration at that very moment, and Henry – inexperienced with tiny newborns – did not act quickly enough, and suddenly baby Hal fell from the king's grasp and onto the stone floor with a horrible *crack!*
Hal let out one sharp shriek just as Katherine leapt forward and whisked her baby up off the floor.
She pressed him to her chest and rocked him gently to soothe him, but the baby kept on shrieking, his gummy mouth open wide in protest as fat tears streamed down his red face.
Henry sprang up from his seat, "What did I do? What did I do...?" he repeated again and again under his breath, his hands on either side of his face, his eyes wide and glistening with fear.
Katherine ignored him and kissed baby Hal's wet cheeks, "*Shhh,*" she soothed, "It's okay, *shhh.*"
With her hand cupped around the back of Hal's head, she could feel a bump forming against her palm, "He hit his head," Katherine whispered anxiously to Henry as Hal's screams began to subside into sleepy hiccups.
Henry did not reply but only stared desperately into Katherine's eyes, silently asking for forgiveness.
The queen inhaled deeply in a futile attempt to settle her nerves, then she gently lay Hal down in her arms and wiped his tears with her hand, "*Shhh,*" she cooed again as she watched Hal's lids become heavy.

"He is going back to sleep," Katherine informed her foolhardy husband quietly, "He is settling. He seems fine."
The words were a relief to Henry's ears, though he heard the disappointment in his wife's tone.

He swallowed his guilt and approached to look into Hal's face, "I'm so sorry," he whispered as he traced one long finger along the curve of Hal's chubby cheek.

"Let's leave him to rest," Katherine said, stepping around Henry, eager to distance Hal from him and his clumsiness.

Katherine's heart ached for her son and the pain he must be feeling, his little head being of no match for the hard stone floor of the castle.

As Katherine lay her sleeping infant into his cradle and his silver rattle above his head, her throat became tight with the unshed tears she was desperately trying to hold back for fear of waking Hal. But more so than that, she did not want to burden Henry with more guilt than he undoubtedly felt already.

And yet the image of her baby falling from her husband's arms kept flashing like a lightning bolt in her mind, the sound of Hal's head as it *cracked* on the floor like a clap of thunder. Henry's naïve haphazardness with their child had sliced right through her, another scar to the ones Henry had inflicted this past year. Though this one cut so much deeper than any of the others.

But it had been an accident. One that could have happened to anyone.

Hal was strong, he would sleep off the pain…Katherine was sure of it.

It was an accident, she continued to tell herself as they watched Hal for another moment, asleep in his cradle, his little chest rising and falling with each breath.

And yet, unbeknownst to them, it was an accident that would cost them dearly.

Having convinced themselves that Hal would sleep off the shock of the fall, the king and queen left in a hurry and without having told the prince's governess anything of the mishap. Hal had seemed well enough, Katherine told herself on their silent journey back to Greenwich Palace.

Throughout the entire journey home, the queen had kept her gaze fixed out the window – seeing nothing – feeling too upset with her young husband to risk looking at him.

He had done many foolish things in the years she had known him, boyish errors made in youthful idiocy.

But *this!*

She would need some time to forgive him.

Though Katherine knew it to have been an accident, an animalistic instinct to protect her child had been triggered by Henry's recklessness, one which Katherine would need to diffuse before she could allow herself to interact with him with any hint of respect.

Upon their arrival back at court, Katherine headed towards the palace gardens, certain that Henry would seek out his friend Charles Brandon to lift his spirits.

"I need some fresh air," Katherine told her ladies.

Catalina and Agnes shared a concerned look, but they did not ask what had happened, for it was none of their business – unless the queen makes it their business.

Which, judging by her irate silence, she would not.

That evening, as Katherine sat before her mirror in her nightshift while Agnes brushed out her waist-length hair, a knock at the door signalled to the ladies that the king was seeking an audience with his queen.

Katherine looked at Agnes' reflection in the mirror and nodded her head lightly, not feeling particularly in the mood to see the king, but knowing she could not send him away.

Agnes hurried to open the door.

At the king's entry, Agnes and Catalina curtsied and quit the queen's chambers to allow the royal couple some privacy.

Katherine remained seated before her mirror, but she met his gaze in the reflection, her face aglow with the flickering of the candles on her nightstand.

"I'm so sorry," Henry whispered as he stared at his wife, his red eyebrows bunched together with guilt, "I feel like a fool."

You are a fool, she thought.

Katherine inhaled deeply and rose from her seat before heading to the bed. She sat down on the soft mattress.

"It was an accident," she replied instead of voicing her thoughts, "He was fine. He is strong and robust. He likely only needed to sleep it off."

"But what kind of father drops his own child?" Henry countered as he began walking towards her, not yet ready to let go of his own guilt, "I should have been more careful."

Katherine did not reply, agreeing with him through her silence.

Henry sat down beside her on the mattress, "I have learned my lesson. Babies are a woman's territory. I am but a reckless oaf. I am not built to handle fragile, little things. Leave it up to the governesses and nursemaids. I shall stick to what I know instead."

Katherine nodded slowly, unwilling to argue with him if it meant he would never hurt her darling Hal again.

They sat in an awkward silence for a while then, staring down at the stone floor before them when Henry turned to Katherine and brushed a lock of her long hair behind her ear and leaned in to kiss her neck.

Katherine closed her eyes, partly in pleasure but mainly in desperation. She did not want to make love tonight.

She wanted to be left alone. She wanted to go to sleep and put this day behind her.

But Henry continued kissing her neck, one hand having come up to cup her breast.

He laid her down and lifted her nightshift, but Katherine did little else than allow him his way with her body, giving him nothing in return, for she was not willing to prolong it.

Henry finished quickly – no doubt sensing her reluctance – and he rolled off her, breathing heavily.

He fell asleep in the queen's bed, his long and muscly body taking up most of it. But Katherine did not care as long as he remained silent so that she could begin to forget this awful day.

Katherine

There is hope blooming in me again.
But how do you pick up the threads of your old life?
It has been two years since his death, and life has gone on, as it does.
There is no stopping the sun from rising, or the leaves from turning brown. Trust me, I have tried.
Life goes on...so in order to not be left behind, you pick up whatever thread you can grab onto, and you pray to God it will lead you into the light.

Chapter 13

22nd February 1511

The following morning, Katherine awoke to the sound of birdsong and a golden sunrise.
She felt better, less irked, and ready to move on.
She imagined baby Hal in his governess' arms, standing by the open window of his nursery, enjoying the warmth of the lazy morning sun on his plump cheeks.
She stretched and turned to lay a hand on Henry's bare chest, "Morning," she mumbled sleepily.
Henry cracked his blue eyes open ever so slightly, "Good morning," he said, before pulling her to him and reaching his hand up her nightshift.
Katherine giggled, "Henry!" she protested half-heartedly before edging closer to him and pressing her lips to his.
Henry caressed her curves gently, slowly trailing his fingertips along the plains of her breasts and down her belly.
He loved that her belly was marked and doughy. It was proof that she had carried his children.
And it aroused him far more than when she had been smooth and unblemished.
They made love tenderly that morning, slow and deliberate with much kissing, touching, and teasing, concluding with mutual cries of pleasure echoing loudly against the stone walls – a contrast of their coupling the night before.
Henry then got dressed and left to allow Katherine's ladies entry, but not before planting one long, lingering kiss on her lips.
It had been the perfect start to the day.

*

Though their morning had started off perfectly, tragedy soon struck, and what had been the promise of a glorious day, quickly turned into the worst of their lives.

Henry and Katherine were sitting side by side on their thrones in the great hall as members of the Privy Council relayed the people's complaints to them.

"There is discontent over the price of bread in –"

Suddenly there was a startled gasp from within the crowd of courtiers as a messenger pushed passed them, "Your highnesses!" he called as he hurried towards them, his face ashen and fretted.

The king was up from his throne in a flash, "What news?" he called to the young messenger.

The man swallowed, his haste to convey the tragic news having rendered his throat dry as a bone.

"It is the prince," he said, and Henry's blood ran cold with dread.

"What about him?" Henry asked, his wide-eyed gaze fixed on the young man before them.

Henry could feel Katherine going rigid beside him, and he imagined she was just as scared in that moment as he was. Perhaps even more so.

"My king. My queen…I regret to inform you that the prince – he is dead."

A collective gasp escaped the court before the courtiers broke out in sorrowful murmurs.

But nothing could have prepared the king for the animalistic howl which would emerge from his wife, a wail so raw and drenched in agony that it would surely haunt Henry VIII for the rest of his life.

Time stood still for Katherine at the terrible announcement, and all she could hear was the sound of her own blood pumping through her veins.

As if in slow motion, Katherine looked up at her husband who stood frozen before her, and she felt suddenly a desire to both lunge at him and cling to him for comfort.

How many scars would I have to justify because I love the person holding the knife?

She rose from her throne then, quicker than she had expected to be able to, and her vision suddenly blurred and darkened.

The people before her became distorted, and she raised a hand to her head in an attempt to regain her senses.

And then she was falling, and she knew she had collapsed by the way the court had cried out in unison, one shrill shriek of angst for their queen.

Then all went dark. And the last thing Katherine thought before she fainted was that she would gladly give her own life if only it meant the restoration of her son's.

*He's dead.
He's dead.
He is really...dead.*

When Katherine came to, she was in her own royal bed with no recollection of how she had gotten there.

"Katherine…"

She turned her head to the side, following the voice, and was met with her husband's desolate expression – and the dreadful news they had received earlier flooded her mind once more. Katherine heaved herself upright, fuelled by her need to know what had happened to her baby, and yet knowing full well that his death had been caused by his fall.

"You did this…" she whispered accusingly at her husband.

"Leave us!" Henry called, to which the queen's ladies and the servants fled the room.

Katherine had risen from the bed, her hood sitting askew atop her head. She righted it half-heartedly.

"He was thriving," Katherine mumbled as she stared at Henry, her voice thick with tears and anger, "He was well. Hal…he was not sick. He was not *dying* until you dropped him!"

She burst into tears then, loud, heartbroken sobs, her face twisted, ugly and inconsolable.

Henry did not reply but only watched as his wife wept, unable to argue with her that he was to blame.

"His governess said there was no pain," Henry told Katherine quietly, as though it were any consolation, "He simply never woke up."

Katherine wailed like a wounded animal at the news. It had not helped her to feel any better, but only aggravated her grief to know her baby boy had died due to a reckless error.

She should never have requested to visit Hal.

She should never have trusted Henry to hold him.

But she had had faith in him. A man so athletic and capable. So dexterous with a bow and arrow…

How could she have known he would not be able to hold their precious baby properly?

Henry was beside her suddenly.

"We cannot tell anyone," Henry whispered then, and Katherine's breath caught in her throat.

She looked up into her husband's grief-stricken face.

"Our baby is dead…your heir…" Katherine countered, shocked by his ability to think past his grief.

He had the good grace to hang his head in shame, at least, and Katherine was glad to see his shoulders beginning to shake as he cried.

They stood there broken-hearted for some time. Both of them weeping for the loss of their child, but neither of them reaching for the other in their grief.

The two life rafts slowly drifting apart in the stormy sea.

"The prince was not sick," Hal's governess, Elizabeth Poyntz told the king and queen later that day as she tried to hold back the tears.

They had returned to the great hall to receive the prince's household, for if there was even a scrap of hope that Henry had not been responsible for their son's death, the royal couple would want to hear it.

"He had been feeding and sleeping well," the governess continued, "as you yourself noticed when you visited yesterday morning – he had been thriving."

Henry swallowed hard then, fearing that the Lady Poyntz knew too much.

"After your royal highnesses left, we had to wake him from his nap to feed. He did take the wetnurse's breast but not as eagerly as he normally did," she wiped her eyes with a handkerchief, "And this morning he simply did not wake."

Beside Henry, Katherine blubbered quietly, her hands covering her face.

Henry cleared his throat, his eyes red-rimmed with sorrow, "Thank you, Lady Poyntz. We do not hold you accountable. It seems there was nothing you could have done."

"The wetnurse did feel a little bump on his he–"

"We trust your word," Henry quickly called, interrupting her before she could finish her sentence.

She looked up at her king, her eyes glistening with unshed tears, and Henry wondered if she really was as clueless as she appeared.

He swallowed his uncertainty, this was no time for taking chances, "As thanks for caring so expertly for our son, I give you an annual pension of £20 for life."

The lady's eyes widened.

"It is the least we can do to show our gratitude for making our son's short life one where he had been cared for and loved," Henry concluded before waving the governess away.

It was a generous gift, Henry told himself, a grand amount of money for someone who had only worked fifty-two days to achieve it.

But Henry could not be foolish about this. Whatever the woman might know or believe, he could not allow her to talk. Hopefully that annual payment would be enough for her to never speak of the child ever again.

Katherine

27th February 1511

It's the day of my son's funeral, and I cannot even attend.
Tradition determines that Henry and I, as King and Queen, cannot attend the funeral of the prince – though we were his parents.
It had been the same for our daughter's funeral, and every other funeral. Though, of course, to not attend this one hurts so much more.
I'd been vaguely aware of the arrangements that had been made.
Hal is to be buried at Westminster Abbey in all the grandeur as that of a Prince of Wales, although he did not live long enough to be granted that title officially.
But what does it even matter?
Whether he receives all the honours of a royal Prince or not…he is still dead.
I imagine his tiny coffin being carried from Richmond Palace down to the Thames where, as arranged, three barges will be waiting, draped in black, to take him up the river.
I had beseeched Henry to pay paupers to pray for baby Hal's soul. He agreed of course, so riddled with guilt is he – and rightly so…
He paid a hundred and eighty of them a handsome fee to pray for Hal.
It gave me some relief. But it did nothing to lessen my heartache.
Prayers will be sung and chanted as the entourage of hundreds of mourners make their way to the Abbey, and thanks to the direction of the wind, I will be able to hear it from where I stand at the open window overlooking the city.

I imagine the tiny coffin being carried into the Abbey, followed by the six knights who will carry the religious and regal banners.

I imagine God welcoming my little baby as he makes his way up to Heaven.

A sob escapes me as I see him in my mind's eye, cradled in God's loving embrace.

At least with the Good Lord, Hal will never again be harmed. He is safe now, in the arms of the One who will watch over him while I no longer can.

"I'm sorry," I whisper into the wind as a tear rolls down my cheek, and I hope Hal's soul will recognise my voice and take it with him for eternity.

As the tears stream down my face, I vow that for as long as I live, I will dedicate my life to my children – if God were to grant me any more. I may have already lost my son…but he will never be forgotten.

No matter what troubles may lie before me, I vow that I will give my all into protecting my children from anyone that might harm them – willingly or not.

Even if it be their own father…

Epilogue:

Katherine

23 years later

June 1534
Kimbolton Castle

  I have been banished and replaced.
Replaced for failing to give the king a son.
But I did.
I gave Henry a beautiful, strapping male heir. As well as our wonderful daughter, Mary, who had been the only light in those dark years that followed Hal's death.
I reside alone in Kimbolton Castle now with only a handful of servants and even fewer ladies-in-waiting.
According to Henry we are no longer – and were *never* – husband and wife…his new entourage of reformers having made him believe that he could so easily be rid of me with only his will.
But God joined us together twenty-four years ago under Holy Matrimony, and it had been lawful then, much as it continues lawful now.
I am still his wife.
Though he parades his concubine about in the Queen's jewels and calls her 'wife', in his heart Henry knows that until I am dead, that honour shall continue to belong to me.
With a flick of my wrist, I send my servants out of my chambers and with the door shut firmly behind them I am now completely alone.
I kneel down beside my bed and retrieve the box I had stored underneath upon my arrival at Kimbolton some weeks ago.

Made of silver and bound on the corners with leather, it is no bigger than a jewellery box, but inside it is the entire world.

I sit on the wooden floor for a while, the box on my lap as I contemplate my replacement, and the life that lay ahead of her.

Anne Boleyn.

May God watch over her in this path she has descended upon. No matter her willingness for this task, she now holds Henry's hope in her hands – and it is an unstable, weak little thing, that hope of his.

How much easier it would have been to simply accept our incredible daughter, Mary, as his heir…

But no, his fragile ego had not allowed it.

I sigh and look down at the box in my lap, my hand resting on top.

It is time.

I raise my hand and I notice that it is shaking as I struggle to open the clasp. It has been twenty-three years since Hal's death, and yet it never gets any easier.

I close my eyes and inhale deeply to compose myself.

I lift the lid of the box – the last time I did so having been when I added an item to its contents eighteen years ago.

I take that item out now: a little wooden poppet dressed in fine silks, a miniature version of one of my own dresses from years ago. This little doll had been my darling Mary's favourite toy when she had been small. I hold the poppet up closely to my face now to try to identify its features, but the years of play have practically rubbed the old thing smooth.

With a sad smile I place the doll on the floor beside me and I wonder how much longer Henry will keep me from seeing our daughter.

Surely now that he has cast me aside and is doing as he pleases with his new faith and following, he could grant me at least this one kindness to see my only surviving child in this time of great solitude?

But I must remain patient. Henry is displeased with me still, as he has been for years – though I have greater reason to be displeased with him and yet I was able to forgive him…

I shake my head. Falling down that spiral of past anger will not return what I have lost. There is no need to squander my energy on resentful thinking.

I look back down at the box, knowing there to be only one remaining item inside it.

I swallow my tears, for I want my vision to be clear and true as I take out the item. Hal's little silver rattle.

I hold it in the palm of my hand, the gift sent from the King of France himself for my son's christening.

It is smaller than I remember. But despite its size, this little object holds more memories than I dare to dream.

In an instant I can smell the sweet aroma of Hal's newborn skin, a mixture of milk and honey. It encircles me as though he were right here in my arms.

The bright orange bushel of curls on his head is fresh and clear in my mind's eye, as if I'd only just seen him yesterday. A tear falls down my cheek – one of a million – though I had tried so hard to contain I;, and before I know it, the rattle in my hand is impossible to see through the outpour of my grief – a grief that continues as raw and tender as a brand-new wound.

I allow my sorrow to engulf me as I rock myself gently back and forth with only my babies' toys for company.

And as the sun descends over the horizon and my tears run dry, I allow myself to imagine the life that could have been.

End of the 'Tudor Heirs Series'

Author's note:

This book marks the end of the 'Tudor Heirs Series', and what a wild ride it's been!
I remind the reader, once more, that my work is fiction, though I stayed as factual with this book as possible since I believe baby Hal's story is important to remember.

One alteration I did make was Henry VIII's direct cause of Hal's death – there is of course no proof of this ever happening. Historians are in agreement that Henry Duke of Cornwall died of SIDS (sudden infant death syndrome), though we will never know for sure.

I tried to capture Katherine's sorrow as well as I could by giving the reader some insight into her thoughts in between some of the chapters where she talks about her grief after losing baby Hal. Those moments, I believe, were crucial to remind the reader from the start that while we are discussing Katherine and Henry's love story, this book was dedicated to the son she had lost – though I had a bit of fun in deceiving you to believe that she was talking about Arthur for a while.
Going back over those paragraphs now you will hopefully see a little clearer that they are the moments after Hal's passing, hence the *italics* to suggest a different timeline.

Writing the 'Tudor Heirs Series' has been an absolute joy! One I have all of you to thank for!
Your support and kindness will never cease to amaze me, and though this series has come to an end, I have many more books to come in the future.

If you enjoyed this or any of my other books on Henry VIII's children, please remember to leave a kind review on Amazon or Goodreads.

www.ingramcontent.com/pod-product-compliance
Ingram Content Group UK Ltd.
Pitfield, Milton Keynes, MK11 3LW, UK
UKHW041312301224
3892UKWH00034B/129